Behind the Mask: Understanding and Healing Male Depression

Behind the Mask: Understanding and Healing Male Depression

TABLE OF CONTENT

Foreword

Depression is one of the most common and devastating mental health issues facing both men and women today. However, men suffer uniquely when depression strikes. The socialization and messaging boys receive about masculinity from an early age—to "man up," to hide vulnerability—conspires to make seeking help profoundly difficult. These masks of masculinity stay with men as they grow older, walling them off from social support, healthy coping, and life-saving treatment. It is time we look behind these masks.

In *Behind the Mask: Understanding and Healing Male Depression*, Dr Monday Farouq performs a tremendous public service by bringing the interior world of depressed men into sharp focus. With compassion born of wisdom and decades of experience, Dr. Monday illuminates the psychological mechanisms that underpin the visible tips of male despair—substance abuse, anger, risk taking, and tragically, suicide. The data do not lie. Male suicide rates are three to ten times higher than females in every age group. For males 15-24, suicide is the SECOND leading cause of death. What suffering lurks behind these harrowing statistics?

Dr. Farouq takes us on a journey to find out. He neither absolves nor blames men for any "failure" to conform to gender ideals. Rather, he traces with a surgeon's precision the deep roots of male distress—biological, developmental, and sociocultural. Modern masculinity was forged in the crucible of evolution to confer survival advantages. But today, Dr. Farouq argues, outdated modes of male socialization serve only to isolate men from each other and from much needed support systems.

Importantly, Dr. Farouq helps men re-define strength and vulnerability so they are no longer mutually exclusive. Asking for help when one is suffering takes tremendous courage. The capacity to listen to one's inner world with compassion and mindfulness takes hard work. These are strengths. And they are the keys to healing.

With expert analysis of clinical best practices, Dr. Farouq empowers men to break free of limiting gender straitjackets and rewrite their own stories. He envisions a society where men can express the full range of human emotions without shame. Only when men uncover and give voice to depression's shadowy presence in their inner worlds, will we finally step out of the darkness.

The time is now. This powerful book sounds a clarion call to action—for clinicians and lay readers alike. We must reach the men who are hurting, isolated and silent. We must provide hope, help and healing.

For anyone who has felt hopeless in the depths of depression, know that you are not alone. Remain steadfast. There is light ahead. For those with a father, brother, son or friend suffering—reach out your hand. Lead them gently to the rich resources in this book and elsewhere. Our culture must change. Let it begin with each of us. We need more understanding, compassion and connection. We need more open minds and open hearts.

Behind every mask is a human spirit yearning to be seen. Our minds may forget this truth, but our souls know it intrinsically. Healing happens in community, by sharing vulnerabilities and finding common ground. In this spirit, we thank Dr. Farouq for a book that will save lives, heal families, and bring men in from the cold. Behind the mask is light, behind the mask is hope. May we find the courage to see it, in ourselves and in each other. The journey of a thousand miles begins with one step. Let us take the next step together.

Introduction

John clutched his sweaty palms together as he sat in the tiny counseling office. "I feel anxious all the time," he said softly, eyes downcast. "I can't sleep. I can't focus at work. I've even had some suicidal thoughts." The last words came out in a whisper.

The counselor, a woman in her mid-forties, leaned forward. "Thank you for sharing this very private experience with me, John. I know it's not easy for you. How long have you been feeling this way?"

John shifted in his seat. "I guess around 6 months. Since my wife left me. But I haven't told anybody. I don't want people to think I'm weak or unstable. I'm supposed to have it all together, you know?"

The counselor nodded. "Because you're a man."

"Yeah." John pursed his lips, eyes glistening. "I'm supposed to be strong. The rock. I have two kids who are depending on me." His voice cracked.

"It sounds like you've been carrying a tremendous weight on your shoulders for quite some time," she said gently.

At this, John finally allowed the tears to flow. His shoulders shook as he released layer upon layer of shame, loneliness and anguish. The counselor handed him a box of tissues and waited patiently for the storm to pass.

After what seemed an eternity, John composed himself. He dabbed his swollen eyes and took a deep breath. "I apologize. I don't know what came over me," he said gruffly.

"You have nothing to apologize for, John. Crying is a healthy expression of emotion. I'm glad you feel comfortable enough here to let your feelings out."

John managed a weak smile. "Yeah well, don't get used to it." They both chuckled.

"One step at a time," said the counselor.

John's story is all too common. Underneath a stoic facade, many men are privately facing immense pain. Why is this, and how can we help suffering men break free of cultural straitjackets to access much needed support? This book aims to illuminate answers.

The data paint a stark picture. Men commit suicide at nearly 4 times the rate of women, making suicide a leading cause of death for males. Depression in men often flies under the radar, manifesting in less obvious ways like anger, substance abuse, gambling or womanizing. Misdiagnosis is common. Men are far less likely than women to seek professional help or talk to family and friends about their struggles.

What accounts for this drastic gender disparity when it comes to mental health? Why do men "mask" their vulnerable feelings beneath a veneer of strength and silence? Are they physiologically prone to depression, or products of faulty socialization? How can we unearth men's buried pain and encourage healing?

The Hidden World of Men's Emotional Struggles

Though great strides have been made in recent decades to destigmatize mental illness, open dialogue still remains elusive in many contexts. For men especially, revealing psychological struggles runs counter to social codes of masculinity. From boyhood on, young males learn to prize qualities like stoicism, competitiveness, aggression and emotional control. Stand on your own two feet. Don't let 'em see you cry. Be a man.

though male depression has existed from time immemorial, it lurks in the shadows—an unspoken epidemic ravaging men in secret. The external presentation masks the interior reality. Men struggling with depression and suicidality often become masters at hiding their true feelings beneath a veneer of normalcy. None will be the wiser until it is too late.

This book brings the hidden inner world of depressed men into the light. It examines with compassion the intense shame and isolation bearing down on men who buy into masculine ideals of strength, control and invulnerability. Far from signs of weakness, seeking help and admitting emotional struggles take tremendous courage. Healing begins by looking behind the mask and embracing the shared human struggle.

Origins of the Strong, Silent Male

Male gender roles that emphasize toughness, domination of feelings, and self-reliance took root over hundreds of thousands of years of evolution. During humanity's hunter-gatherer period, men who could subdue fear, confront predators, and provide for the tribe were more likely to survive and reproduce. Stoicism served a clear evolutionary purpose.

Gradually, these traits became enshrined as hallmarks of masculinity across cultures. The 20th century saw further codification of masculine ideals emphasizing composure under pressure. Post-war America celebrated the strong, silent father figure shouldering his duties with quiet fortitude. A "real man" was measured by what he could suppress—vulnerability, doubt, hurt.

Of course, humans' evolutionary hardwiring differs profoundly from modern cultural contexts. Male emotional repression may have enhanced survival in the wilderness, but proves disastrous when depression strikes in contemporary society. Healing depends on dismantling outdated modes of masculinity that isolate men and cut them off from support networks.

Why Do Men Suffer in Silence?

Men's avoidance of professional services, combined with under-diagnosis of male depression, make accurate prevalence statistics elusive. However, existing data paint an alarming picture of a vast hidden epidemic. So, what holds men back from getting much needed assistance?

Stigma

Mental illness remains deeply stigmatized in many societies, especially for men. Longstanding cultural biases paint depressed men as weak, defective "failures" at masculinity. Admitting psychological struggles provokes intense shame. Men are taught to handle problems on their own. Seeking help contradicts the masculine script.

Minimizing symptoms

When depressed, men often minimize symptoms and insist they are fine. Displays of strength and control reinforce the masculine self-image. Depressed men convince themselves the problem is temporary or not serious based on a desperate need to appear capable and invincible.

Avoidance coping

Men turn to avoidance coping like alcohol, drugs, overworking, anger, gambling and hypersexuality to numb emotional pain and feel in control. These provide short-term relief but prevent addressing the root depression. Men would literally rather self-medicate than admit vulnerability.

Not wanting to burden others

Men view depression as a personal weakness, not an illness requiring compassionate care. Admitting struggles feels deeply selfish, like burdening loved ones with one's own failure or inadequacy. Depressed men isolate themselves to avoid feeling like an emotional drain on others.

Fear of consequences

For men in positions of leadership or power, admitting mental health struggles may evoke fears concerning reputation, status and livelihood if viewed as "unstable". Keeping up a strong facade seems less risky than seeking help.

Warning Signs Hidden in Plain Sight

Depressed men employ camouflaging tactics to keep up a socially acceptable presentation of masculinity. However, telltale warning signs do leak out, often in ways that conform to male stereotypes. Recognizing these subtle cries for help allows us to intervene. Some common signs include:

- **Anger and aggression** - Irritability, frequent anger outbursts, picking fights

- **Risky behaviors** - Reckless driving, dangerous substance use, daredevil acts

- **Avoidance** - Isolating from friends/family, throwing oneself into work

- **Emotional numbness** - Seeming cold/detached even toward loved ones

- **Violent ideation** - Increased fascination with guns, weapons and death

- **Self-medication** - Heavy drinking, drug abuse, compulsive behaviors

- **Somatic complaints** - Physical symptoms like headaches, pain, insomnia

- **Quiet despair** - Negative self-talk, hopelessness, mention of suicide

Culturally reinforced coping like self-medication, aggression and risk-taking allow men to uphold masculinity ideals while unknowingly crying out for help. Improved awareness helps us decode these secret signs.

Beneath the Surface—True Risk Factors

Male depression cannot be simply explained away by genetics or biological hardwiring. Psychosocial and cultural forces are at play. To help men, we need to dig deeper into the complex interplay of risk factors beneath the mask of masculinity.

Nature: Biological Factors

- **Genetics** – Family history of depression increases vulnerability.

- **Hormones** – Testosterone fluctuations and hypogonadism (deficient testosterone) linked to mood disorders.

- **Inflammation** – Chronic inflammation in the brain associated with depressive symptoms.

- **Brain chemistry** – Low serotonin, dopamine and norepinephrine implicated in depression.

Nurture: Environmental Factors

- **Trauma** – Abuse, neglect, loss in childhood erode emotional resiliency.

- **Stress** – Work pressures, financial strain, status consciousness breed distress.

- **Relationships** – Social isolation and loneliness increase depression risks.

- **Learned roles** – Constrictive gender norms limit self-expression.

Clearly, a complex interplay of biological, psychological and social factors underlies male depression. An integrated approach addressing all levels of causation is imperative. Reductive thinking that pins it solely on genetics or masculinity norms will not suffice. We must examine how nature and nurture intersect in men's lives.

Real Solutions—Healing Approaches That Work

While improving public awareness is key, we urgently need expanded access to clinical services tailored to men's needs. We must foster strong therapist-client relationships rooted in compassionate listening rather than just instructing men to "get over it". Here are some evidence-based strategies for successfully engaging and treating depressed men:

Individual Psychotherapy

- **Cognitive-behavioral therapy (CBT)** – Addresses distorted thoughts and self-defeating behaviors fuelling depression.

- **Interpersonal therapy (IPT)** – Focuses on building social connections and communication skills.

- **Mindfulness-based cognitive therapy (MBCT)** – Uses meditation and awareness practices to manage depressive thoughts.

Group-Based Approaches

- **Support groups** – Reduces isolation through sharing struggles in a judgement-free space.

- **Psychoeducation** – Classes teaching coping skills and healthy masculinity norms.

- **Adventure therapy** – Outdoors activities combined with trauma-informed counseling.

Healthy Lifestyle Factors

- **Exercise** – Boosts mood through endorphin release and sense of accomplishment.

- **Nutrition** – An anti-inflammatory diet and key nutrients like omega-3s alleviate symptoms.

- **Sleep hygiene** – Depressed men often have disrupted sleep cycles exacerbating fatigue and low mood.

- **Stress management** – Relaxation techniques like deep breathing, massage and sauna use.

- **Reducing social isolation** – Joining community groups, volunteering, civic participation.

There is no quick fix or one-size-fits-all solution. We must meet depressed men where they are with patience and compassion. Building trust is paramount before defenses can be lowered. Progress will be gradual, with many small steps forward and occasional backslides. But with consistent support, men can overcome the legacy of masculine norms that have trapped them in isolation and silence.

Rewriting the Script of Manhood

Supporting men's mental health requires a cultural shift in how we define strength and weakness. No man is an island. Admitting we all need help sometimes is part of the shared human experience, not a masculine failure. We must reshape boys' and men's attitudes through modeling vulnerability and normalizing open expression from an early age.

On a societal level, we need honest discussions about depression and suicide across our institutions - schools, sports teams, offices, places of worship. Silence breeds stigma. There are also calls to establish a National Men's Health Network modeling the existing structures for women's health. Some argue the general term "mental health" does not resonate with men, hence efforts to promote "men's health" could increase engagement.

Terminology debates aside, the bottom line is we need male-centered spaces and targeted services that make emotional struggles feel germane. Issues like work stress, divorce, unemployment and retirement require a gender-aware lens. Outdated norms equating manhood with self-sufficiency deprive men of needed resources.

Expanding men's help-seeking comfort zone remains an ongoing challenge.

We all have a role to play in creating a culture that empowers vulnerability and dismantles shame. The work begins at home, in our daily interactions with fathers, brothers, husbands, sons and friends. It continues in our policies, institutions and creative output. Men's hidden suffering will only end when healthy masculinity norms take root through relentless, collective effort across all levels of society.

This book provides an intimate window into the seldom-seen inner landscape of male depression. By understanding its layered origins and nuances, we hope to foster compassion, chase away stigma, and show men they are never truly alone. Healing is Possible. It starts with opening up dialogue and building trust. Through courage and connection, men can emerge from behind the masks to live full, authentic lives aligned with their values. The time is now.

Chapter 1: The Hidden Epidemic of Male Depression

Jim always dreamed of being a doctor. He excelled in school, aced his MCATs, and gained admission to a top medical school. His future seemed bright. But within months of starting the intense program, Jim grew despondent. He had trouble concentrating in lectures. His thoughts grew dark, invaded by a sense of hopelessness. Jim stopped attending classes and spent days locked in his room. He told no one, insisting nothing was wrong when friends asked with concern about his sudden absence.

Six months later, Jim took his own life. He left no explanation. Everyone was shocked. Jim had so much potential, talent and life ahead. But under the surface, he was drowning in an invisible storm of depression. Despite his friendly, easygoing nature, Jim never let on about his inner turmoil. He wore the mask.

Jim's story is tragically far from unique. Difficult as it is to confront, male depression has reached epidemic proportions. Yet it lurks in the shadows, hidden beneath stoicism and silence. This chapter explores the scope of the crisis, its systemic underpinnings, and the high cost of ignoring men's suffering. Only by confronting the issue head-on can we ignite real change.

By the Numbers: Measuring a Hidden Epidemic

How widespread is the problem of male depression? Hard numbers are difficult to pin down due to stigma surrounding mental illness and lack of comprehensive data. However, piecing together existing statistics paints a sobering picture of men adrift and in distress:

- Men commit suicide at nearly **4x** the rate of women across all age groups. It is a leading cause of death for men up to age 44.

- Roughly **7 million** American men suffer from depression in any given year—but many lack access to diagnosis and treatment.

- Depressed men are **less than half** as likely as women to receive therapy, medications or other professional help.

- Up to a **third** of depressed men exhibit no obvious symptoms. But they have significantly higher rates of substance abuse and anger issues.

- Depressed men miss an average of **5 weeks** of work due to untreated illness. Job loss often follows, exacerbating financial stress.

- After relationship problems and job stress, the highest predictor of male **suicide** is clinical depression going unrecognized and untreated.

- Approximately **30,000** American men die by suicide every year. It is the **7th** leading cause of death for U.S. males.

While females attempt suicide more often, males die by suicide at a much higher rate due to more lethal means such as firearms. Clearly, beneath the cloak of silence around men and mental illness lurks a crisis of staggering proportions. How did we get here, and where do we go from this point?

Cultural and Social Factors Behind the Male Depression Epidemic

Gender norms play a significant role in obscuring men's suffering. Qualities like strength, stoicism and self-reliance get drilled into males from boyhood. Social stigma prevents many men from divulging emotional or psychological struggles—even to loved ones. Beneath the façade of masculine invincibility resides deep loneliness and distress.

Other social dynamics also contribute to the worsening epidemic of male depression and suicide:

Declining Social Connections

- Men's friendships tend to lack emotional depth and intimacy. Isolation increases when physical proximity decreases after school.

- Marital strains or divorce can completely cut off men's primary emotional relationship. But men re-partner less often than women after a split.

- Widening gender gap in college enrollment and workplace participation reduces male social integration.

Economic Pressures

- Men still feel societal pressure to be the breadwinner. Unemployment and financial strain erode masculine self-worth.

- Workaholism cuts into family time in the quest for status and wealth at all costs. Men pay the price in neglected health.

- Middle-aged male unemployment can be catastrophic, with many skilled laborers displaced by tech advances. Re-training options are limited.

Media and Pornography

- Media images linking manhood to power, dominance and hypersexuality breed emptiness, anger and unhealthy attitudes.

- Easy access to extreme online pornography warps boys' early sexual development and socialization. Objectification and addiction ensue.

- Violent media and video games normalize aggression, risk-taking and a lack of empathy as "masculine".

Barriers to Mental Health Services

- Many men view therapy as too "touchy-feely" and stigmatize psychiatry as just "doping up" with drugs.

- Individualized therapy is at odds with male preferences for problem-solving and group shoulder-to-shoulder activities.

- A lack of male therapists and targeted services stymy help-seeking. General mental health resources feel irrelevant.

Clearly, a cocktail of cultural influences, economic uncertainty, weak social ties and barriers to care converge to damage male mental health. With problems so deeply rooted at the societal level, where do we even begin?

The High Costs of Ignoring Male Depression

It will likely come as no surprise that ignoring the crisis of male depression, suicide and mental illness portends grave consequences:

Human Cost

- Loss of irreplaceable human lives that leave behind grieving families and communities. The tragic waste of human potential.

- Cumulative trauma when boys grow up fearful of showing weakness or seeking help, perpetuating the cycle.

- Physical health impacts of untreated depression - increased cardiovascular disease, obesity, inflammation, immunity impairment.

Family Costs

- Mental illness destroys marriages and stable family structures. Children suffer long-term effects from inadequate parenting.

- Domestic abuse rises when men lack healthy coping skills for anger, stress and depression. Violence harms whole families.

- Substance abuse by depressed fathers sets a destructive example. Sons of problem drinkers are 5 times more likely to develop alcoholism.

Economic Costs

- Depressed men have significantly higher rates of absenteeism and lower productivity at work. Unemployment often results, fueling financial problems.

- Up to 80% of people with severe depression cannot work during episodes of active illness. Many end up relying on disability.

- Mental illness costs the global economy an estimated $1 trillion per year in lost productivity. It hinders human capital formation.

Societal Costs

- Suicide hotlines, emergency responders, hospitals - all strained by the rising demand linked to male suicide.

- Homelessness, crime and incarceration rates escalate in relation to untreated mental illness, especially among men.

- Next generation of boys and young men grow up thinking psychological struggles are shameful, breeding stigma and silence. The cycle continues.

Clearly, the price we pay for ignoring the male mental health crisis is already devastatingly high—and rising annually. The time for action is now. The remainder of this book focuses on solutions by understanding the layered causes, creating targeted services, and reshaping cultural narratives around masculinity and mental illness head-on. The future depends on it.

Digging Beneath the Surface: The Roots of Male Distress

Evolution and Male Emotional Regulation

Gender differences in depression have biological roots in our hunter-gatherer past. Evolutionarily, men who could endure stress without succumbing to paralyzing fear or sadness were better able to provide for their clan and against threats. Stoicism served a survival purpose.

This emotional resilience came at a price - isolation from vulnerability and intimacy. But in prehistoric times, male stoicism increased chances for mating opportunities and passing on genes. Male brains evolved to regulate emotions, especially uncomfortable ones, more tightly. Suppressing was superior to expressing.

Gender divergence in brain structure and function reflects this ancient inheritance. The male brain devotes more real estate to modulating emotions through top-down control, rather than bottom-up emotional generation from the limbic system. Hence men's lower observed rate of anxiety disorders. But this also renders truly vulnerable emotions more alien.

Depression: The Vulnerability Beneath

Herein lies the tragedy - despite men's evolutionary wiring for resilience, depression remains an equal opportunity affliction. When it strikes, men's tightly regulated limbic systems make them especially unequipped to manage the sudden flood of distress. Their masculine armor backfires.

In a cruel twist of fate, the very same neural circuitry that protected our male ancestors from crippling anxiety also inhibits modern men from adequate emotional processing when depression hits. They become trapped in obsessive rumination without the bottom-up skills to constructively reflect or ask for help. A short-term evolutionary advantage becomes a liability.

Socialization: Compounding the Biological Vulnerability

As we've seen, male brains differ inherently from female brains in emotional processing and control mechanisms. But social and cultural forces also conspire from boyhood on to boost stoicism and suppress vulnerability—compounding the biological vulnerability.

Messages bombarding boys from parents, coaches and the media reinforce that big boys don't cry. Be a man. Suck it up. Constrictive gender roles twist emotional vulnerability into a moral and masculine failure rather than part of shared human experience. This social straightjacket gets internalized as part of male identity.

Later in adulthood, it tightens further when depression descends. Seeking help violates every norm of manhood boys absorb through continual repression of vulnerability. Men's layered biological and cultural training fuse together, preventing escape from the inner darkness.

Why It's So Hard for Men to Talk About Depression

Societal norms dictating male invulnerability run deep. How exactly do these forces manifest when men experience depression, leading them to stay silent and bottle up emotional pain?

Gender Role Conflict

Men quite literally perceive seeking help as a violation of their masculine identity. Gender norms fuse to biological wiring, making admitting struggle feel like surrender of manhood itself. Depressed men are trapped in an impossible situation, terrified others will see their weakness.

Stigma of Mental Illness

Even as stigma around mental illness decreases in society, significant barriers persist. For men, stigma compounds with gender roles. Admitting depression feels like doubly failing as a man. Harsh self-judgment blocks openness.

Minimizing Symptoms

Avoidance and denial run high in depressed men. They convince themselves that muddling through with cursory effort is working, that the problem "isn't that bad". Who wants to admit his entire sense of worth has collapsed?

Isolating from Support

When depression descends, men tend to isolate themselves from needed social support. They view reaching out to friends and family as an undue burden, or evidence of failure. Suffering alone feels safer.

Self-Medicating Behaviors

Depressed men often resort to destructive escape outlets like drugs, alcohol, anger, gambling and compulsive behaviors. These strategies provide temporary distraction and a façade of control - but never address core issues.

Lack of Emotional Awareness

Many men have poor understanding of their own internal emotional landscape due to lack of practice and rigid conditioning. Naming and discussing feelings seems pointless, even dangerous to masculine identity.

Fears About Consequences

For men in powerful or high-profile roles, admitting mental health struggles risks stigma, mockery and loss of status or employment. Maintaining a strong image feels less professionally risky than honesty.

Distrust of Therapeutic Process

Male socialization emphasizes competition, status and problem-solving. The softer "touchy-feely" world of therapy, with its focus on vulnerability and intimacy, clashes with masculinity norms.

Clearly, the intersection of biological and cultural forces conspires to keep men silent and isolated when depression strikes. Overcoming these profound barriers constitutes no small task. But solutions begin by naming problems without judgment, and understanding the complex roots of men's suffering. Preserving the status quo is not an option.

Masculine Justice - Rewriting Societal Rules

We must transform outdated rules of manhood that prevent men from receiving care. No one deserves to suffer unaided. Here are principles for a more just conception of masculinity:

- Redefine strength as courage to be vulnerable when facing life's inevitable challenges.

- Normalize expressions of emotion in men as part of shared human experience - not signs of weakness.

- Foster connection and intimacy between men to provide social support and understanding.

- Encourage boys and men to develop emotional awareness and vocabulary without shame.

- Validate that needing help and support does not diminish one's masculinity or value.

- Promote stories of men modeling healthy masculinity, such as seeking therapy during hard times, to inspire others.

- Reform male socialization that frames emotional repression as morally mandatory for respectability and "being a man".

- Make clinical outreach more male-inclusive by training providers in male-specific mental health issues and gender competency.

- Increase male therapists who model emotional skills. Male clients often express preferences for exploring vulnerability with fellow men.

- Demand media stop exploiting harmful male stereotypes. Foster positive role models instead.

By reconstructing masculinity from the ground up, we can create a more just, nurturing culture where boys evolve into emotionally whole men, unafraid to express humanity's full spectrum. The hidden epidemic of male depression demands nothing less.

Chapter 2: The Mask of Masculinity

Brett was a star college quarterback headed for a lucrative NFL contract. He had a beautiful girlfriend, tons of friends, and a rich social life. On the surface, it looked like Brett had it all. But behind closed doors, he wrestled with constant feelings of emptiness and self-doubt. Most nights, he drank himself to sleep just to quiet the negative voice in his head telling him he wasn't good enough. He drove himself ruthlessly on the field to prove his worth.

One day during practice, Brett took a nasty hit that sidelined him with a concussion. As he sat isolated in his dark dorm room recovering, his inner demons emerged with a vengeance. Without football to shore up his masculine identity, Brett's entire sense of self collapsed. He grew deeply depressed and began having suicidal thoughts. But he told no one about the depths of his despair. How would it look if the campus star couldn't just man up and shake this off? Two weeks later, his concerned roommate found Brett after he had hanged himself.

Brett's hidden suffering reveals a common tragedy - men socially conditioned to derive their value from external success and a veneer of strength. When life cracks that façade, the emptiness behind it consumes everything. Yet the mask remains to the end.

This chapter delves into the pressures and paradoxes of modern masculinity - how it inhibits authentic self-expression, fosters disconnection and distress, and prevents men from seeking help when depression descends. Healing involves unveiling the true human being dwelling behind the suffocating masculine mask.

The Top Pillars of Manhood

What defines "being a man" in modern society? Certain ubiquitous messages bombard boys from childhood:

- Conceal vulnerable emotions - crying conveys weakness

- Dominate opponents and display toughness

- Never back down - tenacity denotes true masculinity

- Excel at competition - achievement brings admiration

- Shoulder burdens stoically - real men handle problems alone

- Fight and control inner "weaknesses" - don't give into despair

- Have power over people and events - being a leader commands respect

These stereotypical masculine ideals fuse together, crafting an internalized code of conduct and source of self-worth. But cracks form when life throws curveballs men feel ill-equipped to handle.

When Masculine Armor Backfires

Social ideals that equate manhood with emotional invincibility set men up for isolation when challenges arise. Consider the following examples:

- A man fired from his job feels ashamed that he cannot support his family as a provider. He hides his unemployment and pretends to go to work each day.

- A man's wife asks for a divorce. Rather than admit heartbreak, he buries himself in work and anger while turning to alcohol each night.

- A man's father dies unexpectedly. But he must continue functioning stoically as the patriarchal pillar people rely on, while secretly falling apart.

- A man realizes his marriage is unfulfilling and empty. But he suppresses this, believing real men commit to duty without complaint.

In each case, the masculine script teaches men to keep pretending, keep hiding, keep soldiering on alone. Social expectations create an untenable bind - suffer silently, or cease "being a man".

Negative Effects on Men's Health

Constrictive masculine ideals exact a steep toll on physical and mental health:

- **Cardiovascular disease** - Men have more than 2x the heart attack risk of premenopausal women. Extreme stress is a major factor.

- **Substance abuse** - Men abuse drugs and alcohol at far higher rates. Self-medication provides temporary escape at a heavy cost.

- **Unhealthy risk-taking** - Impulsive danger-seeking allows men to "prove" machismo. But injuries and death ensue.

- **Accidents** - Male risk-taking also leads to higher rates of accidental death via driving, sports, and occupational hazards.

- **Violence** - Men commit over 85% of homicides and are 10x more likely to go to prison. Toxic aspects of masculinity fuel aggression.

- **Reluctance to visit doctors** - Men are far less likely to get preventative care, creating opportunities for preventable problems to escalate.

Clearly, masculine ideals defined by stoicism, aggression, risk-taking, and dominance foster choices with harmful long-term consequences. Yet from boyhood on, boys learn that suppressing vulnerability and pain makes you a man.

"Boys Don't Cry" - Messages Young Males Absorb

Well-meaning parents, teachers, coaches and other role models passively transmit rigid gender roles to boys from early childhood:

- Big boys aren't afraid of anything! Man up and shake it off!

- Don't be a sissy. Stop with the sniffles and whining.

- Crying is for girls. Are you a girl? Only girls tattle and can't handle things themselves.

- Real men don't have feelings. Now quit moping and get back out there.

- Boys play rough. A few cuts and bruises toughen you up. Don't be a wimp.

- Asking for help means you're weak. Just handle it yourself using your head.

Even small comments questioning boys' toughness become internalized as proof of inadequacy. This conditions men to go through life denying vulnerability and struggling alone.

Behind Closed Doors - The Act Gets Exhausting

In public, many men successfully perform the masculine role expected of them - strong, capable, unwavering. But behind closed doors, the effort takes an immense toll:

- Maintaining an appearance of having everything under control requires constant vigilance and stress, even if their life is in chaos.

- Hiding problems and struggles from friends and family isolates them from needed support.

- Suppressing the full spectrum of human emotions leads to bottled up anger, sadness and fear lurking beneath the surface.

- Pretending to be invincible leaves them unequipped to handle life's curveballs when they arise.

- Substance abuse, overwork, gambling and other unhealthy escapes become coping mechanisms to keep up appearances.

- The cumulative impact leaves men emotionally drained and secretly afraid their façade will crumble one day.

In short, masculine expectations based on shame, silence and self-reliance inflict deep wounds beneath the superficial veneer men present to the world. Healing involves bringing these inner wounds into the light.

Why Men Fear Dropping the Mask

Men's extreme reluctance to show vulnerability has systemic roots:

- Childhood lessons equating openness with weakness become embedded in their self-concept and social navigation skills.

- Displaying vulnerability contradicts core masculine ideals like strength, control, and emotional resilience. It feels like defeat.

- They worry showing the "real me" will undermine their career, social status and ability to attract a mate.

- Admitting mental health struggles may lead to stigma and discrimination from colleagues if seen as unstable or incapable.

- Concerns that people will become uncomfortable and distance themselves if negative emotions are expressed openly.

- If they open the floodgates, the breadth of suppressed despair and pain will overwhelm others.

- Fears they lack the skills to healthily process the avalanche of emotions after a lifetime of repression.

- Anxiety over appearing needy, pathetic or defective if they share their true interior landscape.

Make no mistake, these fears are valid. Social stigmas, lack of emotional skills, and the sudden rush of exposing a hidden reality all pose challenges. But living behind a mask slowly suffocates men's spirits. Expanding authentic self-expression and connection constitutes the path out.

Escaping the Man Box

Freeing men from narrow masculine constraints requires dismantling the invisible man box society builds around them. Here are steps men can take to grow into full humanity:

1. Develop self-awareness - Pay closer attention to suppressed emotions that bubble beneath the surface. Be radically honest with yourself about what you feel behind the facade.

2. Get comfortable expressing vulnerability - Open up incrementally to trusted friends and allies. Small steps of risk-taking build emotional muscles.

3. Question limiting messages - When confronted with restrictive gender norms, consciously ask yourself if they serve your well-being. Replace with healthier attitudes.

4. Allow full emotional range - Let go of resistance to parts of yourself deemed conventionally "feminine". Things like nurturing, gentleness, and asking for help are human strengths.

5. Imagine alternatives - What would your life look like if you defined manhood on your own terms? What rules could you re-write?

6. Seek professional support - Therapists provide judgement-free spaces to unpack learned behaviors and build self-compassion.

7. Find healthy male role models - Observe men who embody emotional openness and disregard rigid ideals. Let them inspire you.

8. Speak your truth - Tactfully challenge the problematic "man box" norms you encounter using logic and your lived experience.

The constraints of masculinity loosen one small step at a time. Have courage to walk your own path, define yourself, and surround yourself with others who uplift your humanity. Freedom awaits.

Stoicism - The Gravity of the Silent Man

Of all the masculine ideals discussed so far, stoicism may be the most culturally ingrained and psychologically crippling. Men learn early that the rugged, silent protagonist is heroic. Strong men suffer without complaint or assistance. This edict cuts men off from social connection and breeds grave illness.

Historical Origins

Stoicism arose in ancient Greece as a virtue philosophy promoting composure and self-control. It later merged with Roman concepts like duty and emotional restraint. Stoicism had adaptive benefits in turbulent times - but proved too rigid for flourishing. Nevertheless, Western culture still glorifies the dignified, solemn patriarch weathering life's storms alone.

Why the Silent Facade Persists

Despite its maladaptive effects, stoicism continues to permeate masculinity norms for several reasons:

- Admiration for historical figures like John Wayne epitomizing the masculine ideal of the Marlboro man solemnly lighting a cigarette. The allure of the cowboy riding solo into the sunset remains.

- Cultures that emphasize group cohesion and honor are reluctant to confront problematic dynamics that could stir conflict. Silence maintains harmony, on the surface at least.

- Some men derive a sense of control from toughing things out alone - feeling self-reliant is the true marker of adulthood. Dropping the mask feels childish.

- Cynicism that expressing vulnerability won't be reciprocated or taken seriously. Belief that no one cares about men's problems in a zero-sum gender climate rife with minimized male pain.

Why Stoicism Fails Men

In practice, extreme stoicism proves an untenable and isolating masculine ideal:

- Vulnerable emotions suppressed in the name of stoicism build up unaddressed pressure cookers, leading to destructive outbursts or implosions.

- Refusing help even when clearly suffering feeds feelings of failure and inadequacy - real men should be invincible.

- Isolating from others increases risks of severe depression, addiction, and suicide.

- Relationships remain superficial without expressing authentic thoughts and feelings.

- Physical health deteriorates without proactively addressing problems and practicing self-care.

- Overwork, risk-taking and substance abuse increase in a misguided quest to prove stoic toughness.

Clearly, stoicism once served a purpose but its hazards now far outweigh potential benefits. Healing involves embracing counter-cultural values like vulnerability and connectedness. The gravity of silent suffering must be broken.

Why Men Rage - Roots of Male Anger

Another common but seldom discussed manifestation of masculine distress is anger and aggression. Many depressed men exhibit more overt irritation, temper flare ups, and verbal or physical violence than sadness. Why does male depression so often turn to rage?

Social Acceptability

Expressing anger is more socially acceptable for men than vulnerability. A man who cries openly risks ridicule and stigmatization. A man raging gets dismissed as just venting, no big deal. Anger has an outlet, tears don't.

Evolutionary Roots

Male anger as a fight/defense response serves clear evolutionary purposes. Threatening or attacking an enemy protects masculine status and deters aggression. But this primal wiring overactivates when depression kindles a meaningless internal "enemy".

Link to Shame

When men cannot uphold the masculine ideal of strength and control, they feel deep shame. Anger helps disguise shame into a more acceptable masculine display of power when their real despair slips through the mask.

Loss of Meaning

Depressed men often experience a deep loss of meaning and purpose. Rage provides intensity to fill the void and distraction from intolerable emptiness. Adrenaline and rage temporarily feel better than numb despair.

Learned Coping Mechanism

Many men grew up in homes where only anger was modeled as an acceptable expression of males under duress. Healthy coping outlets remain underdeveloped from lack of exposure.

Self-Protection

Belligerence provides protection against stigma and humiliation in a hierarchical male culture. Pushing others away preemptively avoids wounding to their ego if socially ostracized for vulnerability.

Territoriality

When depressed, men often interpret neutral interactions as threats or slights that must be confronted to preserve status. Anger maintains dominance and territorial safety in their despair-distorted thinking.

While anger surfaces for these understandable reasons, it becomes maladaptive when hijacked by underlying male depression. Constructive anger management provides a pathway to healthy catharsis and restored inner equilibrium.

Perfectionism - The Poison Pill of Masculinity

Undergirding traditional masculine norms lies an insidious yet seldom-named culprit exacerbating men's distress - perfectionism. Though often perceived as high standards driving achievement, perfectionism contains dark undercurrents.

Defining Traits

Perfectionism goes beyond ordinary diligence. Key features include:

- Black and white thinking - viewing outcomes as complete successes or failures with no grey area.

- Over-generalization - one failure means overall inadequacy.

- Harsh self-criticism - focusing on flaws and "shoulds" rather than intrinsic self-worth.

- Unhealthy comparisons - feeling inferior to peers and obsessed with status.

- Self-punishment - atoning for perceived failures through deprivation or high-risk activities.

Though often regarded positively by society, these thought patterns prove deeply damaging.

Hidden Wounds

Beneath the veneer of high-functioning perfectionism lurk deep psychic wounds:

- As the focus narrows on rigid standards, inner wisdom and needs get overridden. Joy is lost.

- External validation replaces real self-esteem. Men become puppets to outside expectations.

- Failure and mistakes breed intense shame, since imperfections get equated with overall unworthiness rather than being human.

- Blurred boundaries develop between needs of the self versus society. Men lose touch with authentic desires.

- They increasingly rely on maladaptive strategies like overwork, substance abuse, dominance and bullying in the desperate quest to be perfect.

Healing Through Self-Acceptance

Healing perfectionism requires radical self-acceptance - embracing the whole self unconditionally, imperfections and all. Here are some principles that help counter perfectionism:

- Acknowledge how early messaging and trauma shaped these patterns; they protected you at one time.

- Notice inner experience without judgment vs forcing external standards upon yourself.

- Broaden identity beyond achievement; you are already worthy beyond any metrics.

- Allow imperfection in all its forms - it unites us in our shared humanity.

- Define success based on aligning actions with values, not status or others' approval.

- Instead of self-criticism, channel anger into social change and barriers that fueled the perfectionism.

- Receive support for perfectionism struggles as courageous, not shameful - this is the healing path.

As men broaden narrow identities fabricated to appear perfect, true self-worth shines through. We arrive home to ourselves.

The Plight of Lonely Men - Isolation as Toxic Masculinity

Beneath the facade of masculine strength resides a vast epidemic of male loneliness. Why does loneliness disproportionately afflict men, and what are its consequences? Let's unravel this phenomenon.

Less Deep Friendships

Men's friendships tend to focus on shared activities rather than intimate conversation. Without safe avenues to open up, men conceal rising distress from friends.

Spousal Communication Difficulties

Many men rely entirely on their spouse or partner for emotional needs. But masculine norms of silence hamper mutual support. Couples often exist superficially.

Weak Community Ties

Loneliness increases when local social institutions like churches and unions decline. Men feel adrift and isolated.

Poor Help-Seeking

Men are far less likely than women to join support groups, therapy, or other social outlets when distressed. Suffering alone progresses.

Economic Forces

Financial uncertainty, stagnating wages and unemployment strain male identity as providers. But they feel unable to expose the toll from shame.

Retirement Adjustments

Men often center their entire identity around work. Retirement liquidates social capital and daily purpose. Isolation rises without proactive engagement.

Widower Challenges

Due to shorter male life expectancy, four out of five widowers are males. Losing a lifetime spouse leaves an emotional void.

Relationship Breakdown

Men have smaller social networks to rely on post-divorce. They also initiate new relationships at lower rates than divorced women.

Lack of Touch

Touch starvation plagues both single and partnered men. Cultural taboos isolate men from same-sex platonic touch that could alleviate loneliness.

Illness and Disability

Chronic health problems that impair mobility create forced isolation. But masculine norms discourage admitting hardship.

Masculine Detachment

Stoicism teaches men early to deny vulnerability. But suppressing feelings cuts men off from deeper intimacy and nurturing social ties.

Clearly, rigid masculine norms foster an epidemic of alienation

Chapter 3: Risk Factors and Causes

Brad was a successful corporate manager and devoted family man in his 50s. He exercised regularly, didn't smoke, and monitored his cholesterol. One day while playing golf, Brad suffered a massive heart attack. The doctors were stunned, given his healthy lifestyle. When his childhood was later examined, a key piece of the puzzle emerged.

Brad grew up with a domineering, hyper-critical father prone to angry outbursts at the slightest provocation. Walking on eggshells to avoid the next rage episode, Brad learned to bury his own feelings and hide any imperfections that could provoke his father's wrath. The outside world saw a model son. Inside, Brad's constant state of high alert took a silent toll as stress hormones flooded his body. These scars remained into adulthood, despite Brad's conscious efforts to transcend his past.

Brad's story reveals a common paradox – how silent trauma endured earlier in life resurfaces decades later in stress-related disease. To prevent and treat the hidden crisis of male depression fully, we cannot focus solely on immediate symptoms. A broader, holistic lens that recognizes risk factors spanning childhood, genes, biology, and cultural forces is imperative.

The Biological Drivers of Male Distress

While environmental and social factors play key roles in depression, biological differences cannot be discounted. Why might men face amplified depression vulnerability in the brain?

Brain Structure

Subtle differences exist in male and female limbic systems, which govern emotion. Women's have larger hippocampus and stronger links between emotion and language regions. This fosters expressing feelings verbally as an outlet. Men's limbic systems emphasize top-down control via the cerebral cortex rather than bottom-up emotional flow. Hence, male brains regulate mood by suppressing emotions and trauma. Over time, this suppression becomes the default.

Hormonal Profile

Testosterone, the dominant male hormone, plays complex roles in mood. While linked to confidence and wellbeing in balanced amounts, both abnormally high and low levels of testosterone in men correlate to depression susceptibility. The male endocrine system is more sensitive to fluctuations that impact mental health.

Neurotransmitters

Male brains utilize lower serotonin, a key neurotransmitter for stable mood. Low serotonin associates with loneliness in men and heightened reactivity to stress compared to women. Some scientists speculate this motivates male risk-taking under duress to stimulate dopamine and noradrenaline in compensatory ways.

Lifestyle Factors

Diets higher in processed carbs and alcohol coupled with lower engagement in proactive health practices negatively influence male blood glucose, inflammation markers, gut microbiome and stress biomarkers compared to women on average. This amplifies risk of depression over decades.

Protective Estrogen

Females enjoy a protective benefit regarding depression through the effects of estrogen. By supporting neurotransmitter balance and neuronal growth while reducing inflammation, their baseline risk stays lower through menopause. Men lack this buffer.

Clearly, male biology and associated lifestyle factors lend themselves to mood instability and melancholy. However, cultural conditioning also figure prominently in the gender depression gap. We must consider brain and environment.

The Role of Childhood Trauma

Childhood trauma powerfully predisposes men to depression later in life by instilling core shame, isolation and helpless patterns carried unconsciously into adulthood. Let's explore some ways youthful emotional wounds leave scars.

Emotional Neglect

Being shamed or punished for crying breeds disconnection from feeling states and self-compassion. A lost childhood stunts emotional IQ persisting into manhood.

Impaired Bonding

Distant, overbearing or abusive parents create insecure attachments in boys. Mistrust of intimacy and dependence on external validation take root. This leads men to isolate when distressed.

Rigid Expectations

Growing up in authoritarian homes where minor mistakes provoked severe discipline teaches boys that perfection equals survival. Self-compassion remains an alien concept.

Physical Abuse

Childhood beatings, pain or intimidation wire boys for perpetual hypervigilance against threats. By adulthood this manifests as anxiety, aggression or substance abuse.

Sexual Abuse

Sexual abuse imparts deep shame and triggers lifelong struggles with trust, sexuality and self-worth. Healing the profound wounds it inflicts requires specialized support.

Bullying

Bullying by peers and elders shames boys for deviating from norms. Suppressing authenticity to avoid ridicule becomes instinctual.

Loss/Abandonment

Parental abandonment through divorce, death or neglect creates a void in male self-image. Men subconsciously expect others to eventually leave without warning.

Modeling of Masculine Norms

Growing up with stoic, perfectionistic male role models teaches boys from an early age that displaying emotion is weak and unmanly. Vulnerability gets driven underground.

Clearly, youthful stressors plant the seeds of masculine turmoil that sprouts in later periods of life. Unprocessed trauma fuels the masks men create. Healing involves integrating memories with compassion.

Why Midlife is a High-Risk Time for Men

While teen boys face social pressures, midlife brings a convergence of stressors that strain men's coping abilities:

Physical Changes

Declining strength, endurance and virility are difficult losses for men to endure. Vanity contributes to depression as the rugged invincibility of youth fades.

Career Pressures

Unemployment or stagnation during peak earning years deals a harsh blow to masculine identity. Imposter syndrome spikes amid younger talent.

Financial Burdens

Fixed incomes struggle to cover rapidly rising healthcare, housing, education and childcare costs. Being the traditional provider grows challenging.

Marriage Struggles

One or both partners realize too late that the relationship lacks depth. Resentments accumulate after decades of emotional distance.

Parenting Demands

Dad struggles over new expectations to be more involved emotionally as kids go through turbulent phases. His own father never modeled this.

Identity Confusion

As kids leave home and familiar routines end, men lose a key role organizing their lives. Emptiness from purposelessness sets in.

Retirement Adjustment

Full-time work structured men's days for decades. Its absence leaves a social and achievement void. Depression spikes.

Physical Isolation

Divorce or widowhood strip away the insulating effects of family for homebound men lacking solid community ties and social hobbies.

Caregiving Roles

Aging parents and partners require more hands-on assistance. But male socialization didn't equip men for nurturing under chronic stress.

Clearly, midlife brings a collision of masculinity theory and harsh realities. Unraveling knotted depression requires unpacking decades of cultural conditioning. Rediscovery takes time.

Why Does Depression Strike Some Men and Not Others?

When looking through the lens of risk factors, depression can seem predetermined and inevitable. But protective factors also play a large role influencing which boys grow into distress and which cultivate resilience:

Loving Family Structure

Boys raised in secure, affirming family environments build core confidence and nuanced emotional skills that last a lifetime.

Positive Role Models

Fathers, teachers, coaches and family friends who model healthy masculinity teach boys that strength includes compassion, vulnerability and asking for help.

Developing Non-Academic Interests

Boys discouraged from pursuing sports, arts or vocational passions outside traditional academics miss out on key outlets. Depression rises when their core aptitudes feel invalidated.

Free Emotional Expression

Families who actively listen, validate feelings and discuss mental health openly equip boys to process emotion verbally vs letting it fester silently.

Ethnic and Cultural Pride

Boys immersed in cultural rituals, rites of passage and oral traditions gain identity anchors that stabilize them through future hardship.

Mentoring and Peer Relationships

Adult mentors provide sage counsel and friendship. Healthy peer connections build confidence. Boys avoid isolation.

Self-Reflection and Contemplative Practices

Time spent challenging limiting beliefs, journaling, praying or meditating builds self-awareness to handle stressors before they spiral.

Accessing Nature and Beauty

Peace derived from simple appreciation of outdoors, art, music and animals boosts mood, creativity and life perspective.

The protective factors that foster wholeness stand as pillars for boys to lean on through life's storms. Building them must take priority over focusing on risk factors alone.

Demystifying the Link Between Masculinity and Depression

Constrictive masculine norms clearly fuel male distress. But the dynamics behind this relationship bear deeper examination to catalyze change. Let's explore nuances at the intersection of manhood and depression:

Masculinity Underlies Both Externalizing and Internalizing Depression in Men

When distressed, men either showcase anger and reckless behavior (externalizing) OR withdraw and conceal suffering (internalizing). Both manifestations connect to masculine norms of strength - externalizers fake invincibility while internalizers isolate to cope alone.

Acting "Manly" Increases Men's Depression Over Time

Putting up a masculine front requires constant effort that builds chronic stress. Men who invest heavily in culturally defined manhood have far worse mental health outcomes compared to peers with more flexible gender identities.

Men Draw Depression Symptoms From Masculine Norms

Stoicism, silence, anger, sexual compulsiveness, workaholism and aggression comprise common depressive coping outlets for men - symptoms culturally reinforced as masculine outlets. This masks the underlying disorder.

Men Blame Themselves For Depression Due to Gender Norms

Depressed men are more likely to believe they provoked their despair through personal failure. Admitting illness contradicts masculine concepts of strength and self-reliance. Stigma deter help-seeking.

Hegemonic Masculinity Harms Both Men and Women

Limiting male gender norms don't just isolate men. They breed discrimination against women and minoritized groups. Relaxing definitions of manhood fosters inclusivity.

Subgroups of Men Experience Varying Degrees of Role Strain

Men of color and those of lower socioeconomic status navigate amplified identity struggles from navigating society's dominant white, cisgender, affluent male archetype.

Conformity to Masculine Norms Damps Men's Well-Being Across Ethnicities

Studies spanning diverse populations globally confirm clinging to strict masculine norms consistently predicts higher male depression compared to cultural flexibility and gender equality.

Depression Symptoms Differ By Individuals, Not Biological Sex Categories

While influenced by masculine norms, depression manifests differently based on men's unique life experiences. Biological sex provides limited explanatory power vs psychosocial factors.

Understanding these nuances provides inroads to help men rewrite masculine narratives that compel suffering in the dark. Broadened definitions of manhood must replace old stories.

Economic Roots of Male Distress in Modern Times

While cultural forces like masculinity account for much depression today, we cannot overlook the material roots of male despair in our post-industrial economy. From unemployment to financial strain to workplace stress, economic structures collude to bury men's struggles.

Devalued "Men's Work" Since Manufacturing Decline

Offshoring of factories since the 1970s dealt a harsh blow to men in blue-collar industries. Loss of stable middle class jobs cuts the masculine breadwinner role off at the knees. Yet policymakers largely ignore these men's grief.

Stagnating Wages

Paychecks for the average American man have barely budged in real terms for 40 years. Increasingly unable to support a family on one income, men internalize failure. Many mask pain through long work hours away from home.

Perceived Opportunity Decline for Men

Loss of lifetime employment and pensions, coupled with soaring student debt and credentialism, leave men feeling locked out of pathways their fathers enjoyed to build a legacy through honest work.

Work Precarity

Gig labor in the modern economy offers little of the anchoring purpose, stability and camaraderie provided by steady jobs. Scrambling between gigs breeds anxiety and isolation.

Consumer Culture Eroding Meaning

Corporate messaging tells men happiness lies in purchasing products, status and pleasing external expectations. But materialism is a hollow stopgap for the pain of meaningless work and social disconnection.

Capitalism Breeding Escapism

The relentless pace and pressures of capitalist production blind men to inner wisdom and health. Numbness provides escape. Antidepressants enable worker productivity rather than healing causes.

Disempowerment

Rising inequality concentrates wealth and power in a tiny corporate elite. Average men feel stripped of agency to carve their own paths. Despair is logical when hope for progress dies.

Alienation

Fragmented, formulaic labor estranges men from their soul's calling. Men medicate alienation through entertainment and consumption rather than reclaiming purpose.

Clearly, radical changes in economic structures are crucial to preventing men's suffering. No man is expendable as a disposable worker. Each deserves safe livelihoods that honor their humanity. Until then, despair persists.

Why Men Endure Trauma in Silence

Trauma is a ubiquitous root of male depression. Yet socialization teaches boys from childhood to suppress vulnerability. This breeds a crisis mirrored in shocking data - over half of men never talk to anyone after experiencing a traumatic event. What are barriers?

Talking Feels Like Reliving

Men fear that opening up will unleash a flood of emotions transporting them back into the pain. Easier to press on stoically.

Admitting Loss of Control

Processing trauma means acknowledging powerlessness which contradicts masculine norms. It feels better to pretend being unfazed and in control.

No Safe Space

Boys lack models of other men discussing trauma in healthy ways. How do you open up when social silence teaches this is inappropriate in all male spaces?

Fear of Appearing Broken

Admitting trauma feels like confirming irreparable damage. This would provoke stigma and shame given masculine directives to "man up" and move on from hardship quickly.

Lack of Emotional Vocabulary

Since boys are often shamed for vulnerable emotions, most men lack fluency discussing complex feelings that emerge during traumatic memory integration.

Caught in Survival Mode

Day-to-day survival demands leave little space for men to pause and process underlying wounds fueling unhealthy patterns. Avoidance continues.

It Happened Long Ago

When trauma occurred in childhood, men convince themselves too much time has passed to surface the pain now. Easier to let ghosts lie dormant forever.

Privacy Feels Safer

Opening up about intimacy traumas like abuse or assault resurrects extreme vulnerability and betrayal of power. Private agony feels less exposed.

Hopelessness in Ever Feeling Whole

Many men see trauma wounds as permanent corrupting stains on identity never redeemable through talking. Why bother dredging up what can't be fixed?

Barring a cultural shift, the surface reasons men invoke to stay silent about trauma will persist. But reaching men's hearts - the universal pain beneath these explanations - holds the key.

Helping Men Break Through Isolation

The cold reality is that many depressed men will remain trapped behind masks, locked in isolation until their dying breath. But stepping into the darkness to reach them is not fruitless. Extending compassion plants seeds for a different path. Here are powerful principles we must embrace:

Listen Without Judgment

Skip the interrogation about why they hide depression. Instead be fully present. Welcome the pain into your own heart. Understand their loneliness implicitly.

Start Small

The tiniest actions to include isolated men matter immensely - lunch invitations, forwarding articles, volunteering together. Momentum builds slowly from sparks.

Check Your Assumptions

Do not presume why someone remains silent about struggles. Nuances around fear and masculinity norms are complex. Asking gently about roots and listening intently helps.

Normalize Talking About Distress

Bring up mental health challenges as you would any other health problem. Chipping away at stigma opens pockets of space where men can talk.

Speak to Pain Behind Anger

When encountering male distress cloaked as anger, listen for hurting behind hatred, fear behind fury. Meet their pain with compassion first.

Allow Processing Time

After men open up, don't demand quick solutions. Vulnerabilities shared shift buried energies. Integration proceeds gradually. Honor this.

Don't Take Problems on Yourself

You cannot rescue someone who remains ambivalent about healing. Offer support but draw boundaries so despair doesn't consume you.

Provide Low-Risk Entry Points

Support groups, nature outings and volunteering allow men to access help anonymously and indirectly if formal mental healthcare feels too exposing.

Appeal to Heroes

If traditional healers are too countercultural, identify historical or fictional characters that model healthy masculinity. Use these heroes to inspire change.

On the path to wholeness, we need only take the next right step, however faltering. When men are ready, they will join us. Until then, keeping the light on matters.

Chapter 4: Beneath the Surface - Signs and Symptoms

As we've explored so far, social conditioning leads many depressed men to conceal emotional struggles beneath a façade of masculine strength and stoicism. However, subtle symptoms do leak through the mask. By improving awareness of these clues, we can catch male suffering early and provide support. This chapter unpacks the most common yet overlooked signs of hidden male mental health crises.

Recognizing Symptoms Disguised As Strength

Anger and Aggression

Short fuse, outbursts over minor frustrations, escalating confrontations, intimidating or threatening behavior.

Many depressed men exhibit anger or violence rather than sadness. Outward rage provides a temporary sense of control. Frequently, it's a cry for assistance.

Risk Taking and Impulsivity

Reckless driving, daredevil behavior, unsafe sexual choices, binge drinking, illegal drug use.

Depressed men frequently self-medicate and distract themselves through high-risk activities that stimulate adrenaline, since open vulnerability feels off limits.

Obsessive Focus on Achievement/Drivenness

Relentless overworking, competitiveness, rigid perfectionism, status consciousness.

Workaholism allows men to uphold the masculine provider role, while enabling avoidance of family/social life where vulnerability could surface.

Violent Ideation

Intense focus on guns and weapons, aggressive or violent media content, increase in homicidal/suicidal imagery.

Culturally accepted masculine outlets like firearms, violent games, and dark music provide fantasized control when internal chaos mounts unaddressed.

Self-Medicating Behaviors

Heavy drinking, smoking, recreational drugs, addiction relapses, painkiller misuse.

Substance abuse is a common but destructive escape valve for men to regulate intolerable emotions, feel emboldened, and reinforce masculine norms of invincibility.

Stoicism and Isolation

Concealing emotions, reluctance to discuss problems or seek help, distancing from family/friends.

Many depressed men isolate themselves to avoid burdening loved ones with their struggles, which would contradict masculine ideals of self-reliance.

Recognizing Symptoms Disguised as Weakness

Fatigue

Low energy, chronic exhaustion, sleeping too little or too much, feeling drained.

Depression exhausts mental reserves. Men deny fatigue, thinking it a sign of inadequacy, but the body reveals distress.

Concentration Impairment

Difficulty focusing at work, forgetfulness, reduced productivity and effectiveness.

Preoccupied by inner turmoil, depressed men struggle with tasks requiring sustained concentration. They beat themselves up over perceived laziness.

Loss of Interests and Motivation

No longer finding joy in hobbies, lack of motivation to socialize, neglecting household obligations.

When depressed, men withdraw from activities tied to masculine identity like sports, career, sex. Apathy replaces usual enthusiasm.

Physical Effects

Headaches, back pain, abdominal pain, changes in weight and appetite, decreased libido.

Depression in men shows up physically as 5x increased risk of chronic illness. But men dismiss symptoms as normal aging.

Substance Abuse Relapses

Reverting to previous addictions and dependencies while concealing the problem from loved ones.

Self-medicating resurfaces as men unknowingly attempt to quell depressive symptoms. They feel deep shame over the perceived failure.

Occupational Decline

Tardiness, absenteeism, reduced performance, conflict with coworkers and supervisors.

Depressed men often experience significant declines in productivity, focus, and relationships at work which they are unable to confront.

Risky Sexual Behaviors

Infidelity, excessive porn/masturbation, prostitution, unsafe sex, hypersexuality.

Some depressed men compulsively seek sexual activity to validate their masculinity, feel in control, or bond with others.

Poor Self-Care

Neglecting health needs, refusal of help from others, lack of motivation for basic tasks like cleaning.

Struggling internally, depressed men often stop caring for themselves. They deny needing assistance with daily functioning.

Quiet Despair

Thoughts of passive self-harm, self-critical inner dialogue, and voicing a sense of despair regarding what lies ahead.

As depression deepens, men may reference feeling worthless, like a burden to others, or that life is meaningless - warning signs of despair.

Why Depressed Men Miss Out on Diagnosis and Treatment

Now that we've highlighted potential symptoms, it bears asking - why do so few men experiencing these challenges get into needed treatment?

- Men are far less likely than women to proactively visit doctors for mental health concerns. Annual checkups provide missed opportunities to assess symptoms.

- Because men display different symptoms than the clinical benchmarks, their issues often get misdiagnosed or minimized as routine aging or stress.

- Primary care physicians rarely use depression screenings adapted for male symptom clusters around anger, sexual behavior and substance abuse.

- Even when men schedule medical appointments, they frequently downplay or fail to mention mental health problems that seem unrelated to physical issues.

- Men are still socialized to view depression screening as taboo or unnecessary - admitting struggling contradicts masculine norms.

- With shorter appointment times, doctors focus on immediate issues. Discussing mental health means going beyond the standard script.

- When prescribed antidepressants, men use them far less diligently than women, as taking medication conflicts with self-reliance.

- Without visible signs of suffering, many depressed men fall through the cracks of public health efforts focused on at-risk demographics like adolescents and the elderly.

- Stigma keeps men from availing themselves of support groups and community mental health resources more often accessed by women.

As these barriers demonstrate, addressing the hidden crisis of male depression requires expanding awareness at multiple levels - from promoting public education campaigns to training clinicians in detecting symptoms manifesting as externalizers and internalizers. Catching suffering early and compassionately is critical.

Why Man Therapy Failed to Reach Men

In light of cultural obstacles surrounding men and mental healthcare, Colorado's Office of Suicide Prevention launched an innovative outreach campaign in 2012 called Man Therapy. Starring a fictional therapist named Dr. Rich Mahogany, the website featured videos and downloadable resources all designed to resonate with male preferences. Yet the program saw only modest success. Why?

Humor Reinforced Stigma

Attempts to use wry humor came off as patronizing. The tone trivialized mental illness rather than normalizing it and providing hope. Men felt shamed, not empowered.

Discouraged Real Help-Seeking

Although the program aimed to encourage treatment-seeking, it relied on stereotypes mocking therapy as silly and unmasculine. This deterred men from pursuing clinical support and community resources.

Risk Factors Overlooked

Content lacked integration of the biological and psychosocial factors influencing male depression. But education on origins reduces men feeling blamed for "failing" at masculinity

Individualistic Perspective

Framing depression as a personal weakness requiring solitary effort overlooked the need for building social connections and addressing macro barriers like trauma or lack of purpose.

Absence of Role Models

No average men shared real stories of overcoming struggles. Uplifting live testimonials build hope. Stock imagery implies therapy is strictly for emasculated weaklings.

One-Size-Fits-All Approach

In highlighting universal male tendencies, the campaign missed chances to target outreach by ethnicity, age and background. No man is a monolith.

Superficial Solutions

Recommendations leaned heavily into physical activity and outdoor time without discussing therapy, medication, life purpose. Exercise helps but more complex healing was dismissed.

Ignored Roots of Anger

In sections on male anger, no parallel outreach existed explaining roots of pain beneath rage or healthy outlets. Anger was presented simplistically as bad.

While the intent was laudable, the campaign fell short of providing a nuanced public health approach to reduce shame, educate around origins, model recovery, and spur broad lifestyle changes for distressed men. We still have far to go.

Private Despair - Red Flags to Take Seriously

Men experiencing depression often drop subtle cries for help in private conversations or actions. Isolation has taught them direct communication will be dismissed or avoided. Here are vital red flags signalling serious suffering:

Negativity/Fatalism

- "Nothing ever works out. I'm cursed."

- "Everything is pointless. Humanity is doomed."

- " I have this persistent sense that my time is running out."

Helplessness/Hopelessness

- " I've sunken so low, and I can't see a way to climb back up."

- "I feel trapped in a bottomless pit."

- " All my problems appear completely unsolvable."

Self-Blame

- " If I were stronger, I believe I could overcome this."

- "I brought this darkness on myself. I'm toxic."

- " I think my family and kids would be better off without me dragging them down."

Feeling Like A Burden

- "I don't want to waste anyone's time with my problems."

- "Others shouldn't have to deal with me. I can tough this out alone."

- "I feel so much guilt for being stuck like this."

Suicidal Comments

- " Sometimes I wonder if everyone's lives would improve if I simply disappeared."

- " Wouldn't it be peaceful to fall asleep and not wake up again?"

- "I read about easy ways people can umm...you know. Get it over with."

If a depressed man in your life voices any statements like these, do not simply dismiss them as venting or gallows humor. Have an open and compassionate dialogue. Ensure he feels heard and supported. Share resources gently. Acting to prevent tragedy matters more than fears of insulting him.

Myths and Facts - Male Depression Basics

Despite growing awareness around depression generally, many myths and misconceptions still abound regarding how this widespread issue specifically impacts men. Let's separate fact from fiction:

Myth: Depression mostly affects women. So it's not a huge issue for men.

Fact: While reported rates are lower for men, experts agree this reflects underdiagnosis. Overall rates in both sexes are closer than people realize.

Myth: Male depression symptoms are no different than women's. So current criteria work fine.

Fact: Men exhibit different patterns like anger, aggression and risky behavior rather than sadness. Using gender-biased criteria misses many struggling men.

Myth: Antidepressants are the best first-line treatment for most depressed men.

Fact: While medication helps some, therapy and lifestyle approaches focused on trauma, purpose and connections are essential to help men adopt new masculine narratives. Pills alone are inadequate.

Myth: Depressed men just need to "man up" and stop wallowing. It's a sign of weakness.

Fact: Mental illness arises from complex factors like genetics, trauma, loss, stress and neurobiology. Toxic tropes around masculinity prevent healing, and drive men to suffer silently.

Myth: Male depression is impossible to detect because men always say they're fine.

Fact: Careful observation reveals symptoms like anger, recklessness, workaholism and isolation. Starting genuine conversations allows men space to open up.

Myth: Depression reflects a personal moral failing or flaw in men.

Fact: Depression has clear biological roots in genetics, hormones, brain physiology, and inflammation regulation. Social factors also contribute greatly. No man chooses to be depressed as a character weakness.

***Myth: Men don't need support groups or mental health resources. They can handle problems themselves.**_

Fact: While taught to be self-reliant, men need communities that reduce shame around sharing distress. This leads men to access help rather than remaining silent and isolated.

Shattering outdated assumptions, judgment, and stigma remains imperative to guide more men safely from darkness to light. We all play a role.

A Cry for Help - Understanding Men's Anger

Like other symptoms, male anger often cloaks an underlying well of sadness, powerlessness and isolation. But when expressed inappropriately, it becomes sabotaging - destroying relationships and trust when men need it most. Transforming anger into healing involves unpacking its signaling function.

Consider What Anger Reveals

- Fear about a situation negatively impacting identity, status, or resources.

- Loss of healthy control over outcomes, leading to distress.

- Feeling disrespected or unfairly wronged.

- Envying traits or privileges perceived to be conferred freely upon others but not themselves.

- Enduring repeated dismissals of needs and boundaries.

- Helplessness when faced with problems too large to fix alone, even if never admitted.

Consider Motivations Behind Anger

- Project strength and control when feeling profoundly weak or defeated inside.

- Hide shame, humiliation or embarrassment over perceived failures or blows to self-worth.

- Manipulate or intimidate others as an unconscious strategy to avoid further hurt.

- Release bitterness and injustice collectvd after a lifetime of silencing pain and grievances.

- Divert others from seeing through the mask of confidence to the fear below.

- Punish society for wounds and betrayal endured at the hands of fate.

Responding With Compasssion

- Listen to the hurt beneath the hatred.

- Assume their best intentions rather than projecting ill will.

- Avoid reacting defensively or escalating aggression. Break cycles.

- Establish clear boundaries without severing connection.

- Care for their dignity and humanity despite unhealthy actions.

- Offer unconditional positive regard while discouraging misconduct.

- Remind them of their inherent value when lost in shame and self-loathing.

With empathy and loving guidance, men's anger can melt into grief, forgiveness, humility and restored passion for purpose. This transformation requires deep trust - the kind that need only be restored once.

Why Men Don't Talk About It

When men open up about depression, it is usually a last resort after extended silent suffering. But what fuels this intense reluctance to verbalize struggles and seek help? Understanding these dynamics is key to creating safer spaces for men to talk openly.

Talking Feels Like Failure

Admitting something is wrong contradicts the male script demanding strength, stoicism and emotional control at all costs. Vulnerability equates to defeat.

Fear of Burdening Others

Men feel shame over the idea of dragging down close ones with their problems. They convince themselves it is nobler to suffer quietly alone.

Lack of Role Models

With poor modeling, men often lack the vocabulary and examples to discuss despair in healthy ways. They worry sharing will make them sound pathetic.

Self-Reliant Mindset

Seeking help violates norms of male independence and handling problems alone. Even therapists feel uncomfortably "feminine".

Distrust of Vulnerability

Letting down guard and exposing insecurities to another person feels dangerous. Fears around loss of status and betrayal loom large.

Stigma of Mental Illness

Mental health struggles connote weakness in a man's eyes. To admit depression feels like surrendering dignity and personhood.

Minimizing Suffering

Men tell themselves their struggles aren't serious enough to merit help, that they should just "get over it". Saving face takes priority.

Avoidance Coping

Many men distract themselves from depression temporarily through escapes like work, substances, sex. But denial prevents resolution.

Clearly, the social training and narratives ingrained in men since boyhood pose powerful deterrents to discussing mental health openly, as vulnerability counters the masculine code. We must stand witness and help men rewrite this story.

Ending the Shame Game Surrounding Male Depression

Transforming cultural narratives that trap men in silence and shame requires undoing generations of stigma and redefining strength. Here are principles for fostering dialogue and understanding:

Mental Illness is Not a Character Flaw

Reinforce that depression results from complex factors like genetics and stress - not personal weakness. Men must unlearn equating illness with failure.

Vulnerability Requires Great Courage

Reframe seeking help during struggles as an act of bravery and wisdom, not defeat. Fighting stigma takes resilience.

Emotions Are Part of Being Human

Allow men safe spaces to express feelings openly, without judgment. Suppressing emotions for years causes damage.

Recovery Stories Foster Hope

Spotlight examples of average men who overcame depression through professional help and lifestyle changes. This motivates others that healing is possible.

Progress Over Perfection

Resist holding men to unrealistic ideals around masculine invincibility. Expect bumps along the recovery journey - progress over perfection.

We All Need Community

Normalize men's need for strong social ties. Challenges are too heavy for anyone to carry alone. Offer support consistently.

New Narratives of Masculinity

Celebrate role models who creatively expand cultural concepts of masculinity beyond tired stereotypes that fuel shame.

Accountability with Compassion

Promote taking responsibility for actions without self-blame. Depression explains but does not excuse harming self/others.

With concerted effort across all levels of society, male depression can emerge from the shadows. The work begins with daily acts of understanding toward the men in our lives. Each small step matters.

Integrative Treatment - Mind, Body and Spirit

While undeniably helpful for many, medication alone cannot fully address the layered biological, psychological and social roots of male depression. Holistic integration of professional treatment, lifestyle changes, community support and spiritual practices proves most effective.

Counseling and Therapy

Talk therapy equips men with tools to transform thought patterns, heal past trauma, build self-compassion and strengthen vulnerable communication skills. Finding the right counselor to establish trust is key.

Medication Options

Antidepressant medications help restore neurochemical balance in the brain when combined with other interventions. However, they cannot resolve underlying issues like trauma, loneliness and lack of purpose which fuel depression.

Physical Activity and Nutrition

Regular exercise, taking nature walks, sports with others, and eating an anti-inflammatory whole foods diet have natural antidepressant effects by normalizing hormones, reducing inflammation, and promoting self-care.

Support Groups

Group therapy reduces isolation by creating community and accountability for men working through similar struggles. It helps men adopt vulnerability.

Life Purpose Exploration

Depression often arises when men lack meaning, fulfillment and alignment of work with values. Rediscovering passion reduces emptiness.

Nature Immersion

Time outdoors, especially in green spaces, restores mental health by lowering stress hormones, inspiring awe and encouraging mindfulness.

Journaling

Capturing emotions and thoughts on paper moves them out of repetitive loops in the mind and allows perspective. This builds emotional intelligence.

Meditation

Mindfulness practices train skills to observe thoughts non-judgmentally, enhancing emotional control. Regular meditation rewires neural pathways.

Self-Care Routines

Healthy sleep hygiene, down time, saying no to obligations, massages, and other forms of restorative nurturing enhance well-being.

Clearly, sustainable healing requires maximizing lifestyle factors, community support and meaning alongside professional treatment. No single solution standalone suffices long-term. Integrating all aspects fosters lasting wholeness.

Why Men Don't Come In for Counseling

Given widespread stigma surrounding therapy, many men either refuse to attend counseling when depression descends or fail to stick with it. What key barriers deter men from engaging?

Talking Feels Like Failure

Admitting something is wrong contradicts the male script demanding strength, stoicism and emotional control at all costs. Vulnerability equates to defeat.

Distrust of The Process

The intimate self-disclosure integral to therapy conflicts with male preferences for action-oriented, tangible problem-solving. Just "talking about it" seems pointless.

Fear of Judgment

Men feel apprehensive about being professionally evaluated as defective, unstable or unmasculine due to mental health struggles. Fears of being misperceived loom large.

Loss of Control

The therapist leading probing discussions feels uncomfortably exposing and passive for men used to directing conversations and relationships. It evokes vulnerability.

Stigmatized as Weak

In most male circles, attending therapy remains highly stigmatized as an admission of failure at handling challenges independently and internally.

Lack of Role Models

Many men have no examples of other males in their lives openly discussing going to therapy. The concept feels foreign and emasculated.

Dearth of Male Therapists

The stark imbalance of women among mental health professionals poses another deterrent to men, who express preference for exploring vulnerability with those who share their gender experience.

Quick Fix Expectations

Conditioned to appear perpetually strong, men expect therapy to produce immediate changes. When progress unfolds gradually over weeks, frustration mounts.

Clearly, societal scripts equating masculinity with emotional control and self-reliance breed aversion to therapy's central tenets. We must reverse these narratives to foster healing.

Group Therapy - A Powerful Tool for Men

While counseling brings immense benefits, group therapy provides a key social outlet for men to open up without isolation. Shared struggles build connection and community. Here's how:

Reduces Shame

Listening to other men tell their stories normalizes getting support. The stigma of attending therapy declines.

Builds Trust

Watching peers model vulnerability in a safe, confidential space inspires men to take risks sharing their authentic struggles without judgment.

Provides Perspective

Hearing a diverse range of male experiences with depression helps men realize they are not alone or solely to blame for their troubles.

Creates Accountability

Gentle confrontation from peers when someone makes excuses or minimalizes issues provides reality testing that therapists alone cannot always offer.

Fosters Hope

Bearing witness to other men improve, build skills and recover belief in themselves demonstrates healing is possible, inspiring optimism.

Enhances Communication

Practicing expressing feelings and listening to peers constructively builds emotional vocabulary and confidence men lack. Skills become habits.

Normalizes Setbacks

When group members share their stumbles, backslides and mistakes, it helps men see periodic setbacks are normal parts of recovery rather than failure.

Provides Ongoing Support

Groups offer built-in support networks that persist even after formal treatment ends, providing community during the crucial transition period post-discharge.

Clearly, although initially intimidating, group therapy delivers life-changing impact for men in ways individual counseling alone often cannot. Combining both modalities proves most effective.

Why Men's Trauma Goes Unrecognized

Despite being just as vulnerable to post-traumatic stress as women, men often do not receive needed support due to normalization of trauma responses as "masculine" behaviors. Let's explore why men's trauma flies under the radar.

Anger and Aggression

Outbursts, violence, picking fights, bullying, and intimidating others may be seen as typical bad male behavior rather than trauma responses that warrant compassion.

Risk-Taking

Reckless behaviors like gambling, substance abuse, daredevil stunts, and unsafe sex read as stereotypical rather than red flags that trauma is driving self-destructive impulses.

Competitiveness

Obsession with achievement, perfectionism, workaholism and status are praised in men as ambition rather than recognized as trauma-fueled attempts to reclaim power and control.

Stoicism

Emotional unavailability, isolation, silence about feelings, and refusal to seek support often gets dismissed in men as the strong, silent type rather than a sign they require professional care.

Hypersexuality

Promiscuity, pornography addiction, and infidelity are excused in men as hormonal rather than signals he is compulsively trying to manage flashbacks, loneliness and inner numbness.

Victim Blaming

When men do experience assault, exclusion, bullying, abuse, or betrayal, cultural biases lead to questioning what they did to deserve it rather than offering empathy and concern. Minimizing male trauma as an anomaly or fluke is easier than confronting how profound and widespread it truly is. But this only perpetuates suffering in silence.

Clearly, societal blind spots around men's mental health frequently prevent proper identification and compassionate response regarding male trauma. But by better understanding common trauma responses in men, we can catch suffering early and provide needed support.

Helping Men Break Free of Pornography

For many depressed men, pornography use becomes an unhealthy obsession and escape exacerbating isolation. But practical steps focused on compassion rather than shame can help men break free of porn's hold and restore intimacy.

Understand Motivations

Control, numbing pain, meeting unfulfilled needs for intimacy, and despair over real relationships can all drive excessive porn use. See it as about pain, not pleasure.

Replace, Don't Just Resist

Lethargy and emptiness left from removing porn must get filled with human connection, purposeful hobbies, exercise, time in nature, and self-care to sustain motivation.

Establish Accountability

Trusted friends or support groups providing strength for moments of weakness reduce shame in admitting relapse while building resolve to persist.

Address Core Issues

Past trauma, family dynamics, relationship skills, lack of touch/affection and other root causes must get resolved so porn doesn't fill these voids again when emotions intensify.

Set Healthy Boundaries

If certain stresses or moods tend to trigger porn use, proactively avoiding those contexts until recovery strengthens can circumvent relapse before provocation arises.

Cultivate Self-Worth

Healing core shame through self-love practices like journaling, therapy, and mindfulness weakens porn's temporary emotional escape by filling the void within sustainably.

Promote Vulnerability and Intimacy

Opening up to trusted friends and partners about struggles and hurts fosters the nurturing connections that porn seeks to imitate artificially.

Consider Medication

If obsessive impulses feel unmanageable despite best efforts, antidepressants may provide just enough boost in dopamine and serotonin levels to reduce cravings long enough to do deeper therapeutic work and lifestyle changes.

With compassionate effort focused on healing rather than judgment, men can break free of porn's lure and channel unmet needs in constructive directions. We all stumble; getting up stronger matters most.

Alzheimer's - When Memory Loss Prevents Healing

As men grow older, Alzheimer's disease and related dementias pose particular challenges for resolving undiagnosed depression before cognitive decline progresses. Here are coping strategies caregivers can employ:

Gather His History

Ask family members about his past mood, childhood, traumas, and coping patterns to gain insight into his current state since he cannot provide background.

Note Emotional Changes

Keep observing his mood and behavior for signs of depression like social withdrawal, disrupted sleep, irritability, or sadness and validate these feelings.

Foster Routine

Consistent daily rhythms and familiar activities provide comfort and minimize disorientation triggering depression when memory falters.

Avoid Overstimulation

Too many competing sights and sounds quickly overwhelm the senses, leading to agitation or shutdown. Simplify the environment.

Provide Reassurance

Verbally remind him of your unconditional support and his inherent worth frequently, as his sense of identity and safety dissolves.

Encourage Reminiscence

Looking at old photos, listening to familiar music, and retelling positive memories provide continuity and lift mood.

Check Pain Levels

Unaddressed physical pain often causes acting out. Rule out sources of discomfort precipitating behavioral changes before assuming dementia or psychosis.

Limit News Exposure

Graphic coverage of violence, death, and tragedy feed paranoia and despair. Protect his sensitivities.

Though direct resolution grows impossible as cognition fades, surrounding him with compassionate care tailored to retain joy and meaning amid loss still greatly eases suffering. Where words fall short, love speaks the loudest.

Supporting Male Survivors of Assault

Sexual assault conveys deep psychic wounds for male victims, given cultural biases questioning masculine identity after violation. Supporting healthy recovery requires countering those myths with truth:

- Violation in no way diminishes their worth, strength, masculinity or humanity.

- Responsibility lies solely with the perpetrator; survivors did nothing to deserve harm.

- Male assault is more widespread than society admits; they are not alone.

- Suppressing pain and trauma will only breed greater illness; safe emotional expression is healing.

- Asking for help when vulnerable embodies true courage and wisdom.

- Full recovery may be gradual and nonlinear; be patient with the process.

- Their capacity for joy, intimacy and purpose can fully return in time.

- Shared stories help other male survivors feel less alone; speaking up prevents cycles of shame.

- Though changed by trauma, their power to overcome and thrive rises from within.

- Compassion must be extended first to themselves on the long path to wholeness.

By modeling unconditional listening free of judgment, assumptions and constrictive masculinity norms, caregivers and counselors of assaulted men plant seeds of hope that grow over time into peace.

Helping Men Discover Healthy Intimacy

Depression in men often intertwines with distorted ideas of intimacy that prevent forming nurturing relationships. Here are principles for encouraging intimacy growth:

Explore Fears

Vulnerability feels dangerous to men. What past experiences or messages shaped this? Healing those origin wounds is key.

Define Intimacy Beyond Sex

Expand understanding to encompass emotional and spiritual closeness. These nourish and protect long-term unions.

Challenge False Notions

Popular culture perpetuates myths like men cheat because they are horny and women need saving. How do these skew perceptions?

Foster Friendships

Meaningful same-sex friendships build trust and communication skills that strengthen romantic intimacy.

Encourage Mentors

Positive role models demonstrate healthy relating across contexts like work, home and community.

Unpack Relationship History

Past betrayals, attachment injuries and family dynamics unconsciously influence intimacy patterns unless brought into awareness.

Set Healthy Boundaries

Defining and maintaining clear boundaries builds the assertiveness that sustains intimacy more than passive compliance or anger.

Name Emotional Needs

Men must develop literacy around feelings and asking for nurturing rather than expecting partners to mind-read.

Highlight Green Flags

Healthy intimacy goes beyond avoiding clear red flags. How do daily greens like respect and reliable support sustain couples?

By gradually dismantling dysfunctional patterns and narratives that restrict men's capacity for vulnerability, compassionate bonds can blossom and flourish.

Helping Perfectionist Men Find Balance

The masculine pressures to dominate and achieve imposed by families and society breed perfectionism in many men. But healing over-control and self-criticism involves adopting healthier perspectives:

Separate Worth From Achievement

Like all humans, men have inherent value apart from any titles,
status or accomplishments. What speaks to their deeper purpose and
talents?

Set Manageable Goals

Rather than unrealistic expectations bred by perfectionism,
encourage modest, measurable goals that provide a sense of
progress. Small wins matter.

Allow Imperfection

Progress happens slowly with ample mistakes and lessons along the
way. Model laughing at blunders as teachers, not evidence of
inadequacy.

Recognize Effort, Not Just Outcomes

Praise steps in the right direction and celebrating sincere attempts.
It's about progress, not endpoints.

Push Back Against All-Or-Nothing Thinking

Black-and-white patterns like "I'm a total failure if I don't get the
promotion" leave no room for growth or gray areas. Challenge
dichotomies.

Take Brakes

Perfectionists lose sight of natural human limits and capacity.
Encourage rest, saying no, and deleting unnecessary obligations
from crowded schedules.

Identify Shoulds

"I should be..." self-talk reflects external pressure, not internal
values. What do they authentically want for themselves, beyond
meeting others' standards?

Seek Healthy Mentors

Exposure to role models who hold high standards while remaining compassionate and centered provides a well-rounded example to emulate.

By steadfastly reorienting compulsive striving toward sustainable effort fueled by purpose rather than fear, men transcend the emptiness of perfectionism to embrace human wholeness.

Why Men Struggle to Discuss Feelings

One of the most tragic consequences of harmful masculine norms is the immense difficulty most men experience openly discussing feelings and emotions, even with close loved ones. What underlies these communication barriers?

Emotions Viewed as Weakness

Boys learn early that expressing vulnerability betrays manhood. Suppressed pain breeds isolation.

Lack of Modeling

If male family members avoided emotional awareness and intimacy, boys implicitly absorb stoicism as the way to appear strong like Dad.

Focus on External rather than Internal

Male socialization prioritizes doing over being, depriving boys of tools to cultivate self-awareness and emotional intelligence.

Acting Tough Is Safer

Being emotionally detached and stoic protects against the shame of rejection if they risk vulnerability with peers or partners.

Discomfort with Emotion

If raised in a culture where overt emotion is taboo, even words for feelings sound foreign and uncomfortable when trying to open up.

Fear of Being Harshly Judged

Boys absorb messages that having stereotypically "feminine" feelings like hurt or sadness makes them inferior, reinforcing silence.

Feeling Like A Burden

Men worry expressing struggles and seeking comfort from loved ones makes them a drain emotionally, so they prematurely conclude vulnerability has no place.

Lack of Practice

Without ongoing opportunities to share emotional experiences verbally in boyhood, a steep learning curve faces men trying to access these skills later in life when confronting mental health crises or relationship conflicts.

But despite profound conditioning, authentic communication can be relearned through courage, compassion and commitment to conscious relating. Emotions blocked for decades can flow freely again.

Helping Military Men Admit Vulnerability

The hardcore masculine culture drilled into soldiers prevents many veterans from seeking help when battling untreated depression, PTSD, or suicidal thoughts post-deployment. What approaches get through?

Start Where They Are

Use familiar military touchpoints - courage, duty, honor, loyalty - to reframe strength as getting support and recognizing their sacrifices matter.

Tell Positive Stories

Spotlight veterans who have addressed mental health issues successfully to inspire hope in those still struggling alone. Peers are powerful messengers.

Provide a Safe Haven

Male-only groups held in trusted environments build the vulnerability and rapport necessary before veterans open up to clinicians and family.

Speak Their Language

Relate psych concepts in concrete terms like physical pain, mission objectives, and chain of command. Military metaphors resonate better.

Offer Anonymity

Hotlines, textlines, and online forums allow vets to anonymously "test the waters" expressing struggles without feeling exposed. Confidentiality is key.

Address Shame

Many feel guilt over surviving while comrades died, or shame around trauma responses. Validate these men did not choose PTSD symptoms and are still honorable.

Emphasize Resilience

Reframe therapy and lifestyle changes as ways to regain the strength and discipline soldiers once relied upon, rather than last resorts of the weak.

Know the Triggers

Anniversaries of losses, combat trauma themes in media, fireworks, loneliness during holidays - all can provoke depression or PTSD without warning.

With insight into military culture's pressures and landmines, we can thoughtfully guide struggling veterans and service members toward regaining hope, purpose and community. Their loyal hearts deserve no less.

Preventing Veteran Suicide

With highly regimented training emphasizing brotherhood, purpose and strength, transitioning to civilian life often overwhelms veterans already struggling with untreated PTSD and depression. Comprehensive outreach is key to reducing veteran suicide:

Start the Conversation Early

Address mental health checkups pre-discharge so needs get identified before loss of structure and daily military rhythms send veterans into isolation. Stigma prevents many from proactively seeking help once outside.

Continuity of Care

Ensuring veterans leaving service already connected to psychiatric medication, therapy and support groups experience no gap in accessing these after re-entry prevents crises from deteriorating when stability vanishes.

Lethal Means Restriction

Respectfully ask at-risk veterans to temporarily place weapons or ammunition with trusted individuals during transition or mental health struggles. Many suicides are impulsive reactions during crises. Preserving life comes first.

Family Inclusion

Bring spouses and children to counseling sessions to foster understanding of PTSD and depression. This equips families to recognize symptoms and intervene with love, not frustration.

Peer Support Integration

Connect transitioning veterans with peer-led support groups, sponsors and new mission-driven communities (like volunteering) to replace lost sense of purpose after service ends.

Job Training Programs

The structure of work provides mental health benefits. Services teaching vocational skills, assisting with resumes/interviews and providing transitional employment help instill purpose.

Prevent Contagion After Loss

Special attention and mental health outreach must immediately occur after a unit member's suicide to identify and support at-risk peers. Postvention prevents contagion.

Self-Care Routines

Work with veterans to build healthy daily routines involving sleep, nutrition, exercise, leisure and social time. This provides stability and mental health benefits.

With holistic, multimodal approaches, the transition to civilian life can fortify rather than damage mental health for veterans. But adequate systemic resources and public commitment remain lacking. We must care for those who served.

Police Psychology - Preventing Trauma and Suicide

Similar to the military, the insulating culture of strength, self-reliance and constant vigilance in police forces often deters officers from admitting psychological wounds until it's too late. Some promising approaches to protect police mental health include:

Embedded Mental Health Professionals

Having counselors and peer supporters work alongside police reduces stigma of seeking treatment externally. Help travels to them.

Proactive Screening Protocols

Regular mandatory check-ins assess depression, trauma, burnout risk before crises occur. Annual exams miss emerging problems.

Family Education and Support

Spouses and children can gently intervene when seeing officers exhibit PTSD symptoms at home. But they require guidance to distinguish symptoms from bad behavior.

Routine Mental Health Check-Ups

Like physical exams, promoting voluntary regular counseling tune-ups removes stigma around only accessing services when "broken".

Suicide Prevention Training

Teaching officers to recognize risk factors, safely store weapons, reduce access to lethal means and refer peers to help saves lives during impulsive moments.

Substance Abuse Treatment

Referring alcohol issues proactively through employee assistance programs provides help before addiction progresses. Drugs and alcohol worsen PTSD.

Peer Support Groups

Veteran officers leading sessions fosters trust and understanding around trauma, depression, grief and other struggles faced internally but seldom discussed.

Crisis Lines and Chaplains

Easy anonymous access to counselors trained in police culture offers support without fear of professional consequences. Chaplains provide spiritual comfort.

Mandatory Time Off

Enforced leave policies prevent relentless work cycles that lead to burnout and suicidal desperation. Respite brings perspective.

With courageous culture change from the top down, mental health promotion in police forces helps those who serve and protect our communities get the specialized support they need and deserve. Small daily acts of compassion hold infinite power.

Counseling Men on Anger and Aggression

When men present with frequent anger, irritation and aggression, counseling should compassionately address unresolved hurts beneath the surface:

- Explore the thoughts, feelings and physical sensations anger elicits using mindfulness. This builds self-awareness and pausing skills to prevent instinctual reactions.

- Unpack family and cultural sources imprinting anger as an acceptable emotion where vulnerability gets suppressed or invalidated.

- Identify patterns, sequences and triggers that reliably prompt anger. Brainstorm alternative responses ahead of provocation next time.

- Consider unmet needs anger aims to achieve like control or hiding hurt. What healthier means could foster security and self-expression?

- Assess lifestyle factors like substance use, sleep disruption, social isolation or excessive stress fueling irritability. Strengthen health foundations.

- Offer referrals for psychiatric evaluation if aggression seems continually out of the client's control despite best efforts. Medications can stabilize brain chemistry while doing deeper therapeutic work.

- Note signs of past trauma. Memories and sensory associations often unconsciously evoke excessive defensive rage. Gently addressing trauma reduces exaggerated reactivity.

- Teach calming practices like breathing, nature sounds, mediation, prayer, music, and exercise to manage anger surges in the moment. Coping skills must become second nature.

- Explore false masculine beliefs like "Anger makes people respect me". Challenge notions that bile builds bonds. Anger risks pushing people away long-term.

- Role play assertive communication scenarios focused on "I" statements, listening and compromise. These tools resolve conflict more sustainably than aggression.

- Praise small acts of restraint, non-violence and pausing during anger triggers. Gradually a new self-image evolves.

With insight, skills and compassion for past wounds fueling male anger, clinicians help clients gain control rather than be controlled by this destructive emotion. Support transforms suffering.

Reducing Men's Suicide Risk in Midlife

Given the painful intersection of aging, identity loss and outdated masculine norms, middle age poses high suicide risk for men unable to envision a way forward. Some clinical approaches include:

Screening for Depression

Actively assess midlife men for symptoms like emptiness, fatigue, hopelessness and anger, recognizing depression often disguises inwardly to preserve masculine self-image.

Instilling Hope

Share stories of men who discovered meaning and new purpose after midlife setbacks. At times, living examples inspire more than abstract assurance.

Reframing Circumstances

Guide men to see transition as opportunity for reinvention versus failure. External markers of status and virility inevitably evolve with time. What truly matters most? Who might they become?

Validating Emotions

Permit men space to grieve losses of youth without judgment or false reassurance. Finding meaning in suffering relieves shame.

Supporting Identity Growth

Depression often signifies weak spots in identities built on career status, money, or bravado. Help men rediscover dormant talents, passions and values to rebuild on foundations of character and community.

Encouraging Peer Bonds

Isolation feeds despair's vicious cycle. Beer nights, sports teams, coffee clubs, volunteering provide natural male camaraderie missing since school days.

Cultivating Purpose

Channeling energy into nurturing projects and people fosters meaning. Teach depressed men that contributing to family, charity, careers remains possible despite limitations.

Facilitating Lifestyle Changes

Good self-care like nutrition, nature time, sleep, exercise and minimizing substances provides mental health support while identity shifts occur. Small changes accumulate.

Exploring Medication Options

Discuss antidepressant benefits and side effects honestly while presenting meds as tools in a comprehensive toolbox alongside therapy and peer support. This reduces stigma.

With compassion for midlife's existential crossroads, clinicians guide men through dark nights of the soul into liberating newfound wisdom and purpose awaiting on the other side. There is light ahead if we walk toward it together.

Counseling Older Men on Isolation and Loneliness

As men enter later life, physical limitations, retirement and loss of loved ones breed acute isolation. Some therapeutic approaches that help include:

Validating Grief

Provide a non-judgmental space for men to discuss loss of virility, independence, purpose and peers without shaming emotional needs.

Exploring Social Options

Brainstorm volunteering, religious groups, senior centers or clubs tailored to interests. Taking first steps combats inertia and fears holding isolated men back.

Role Playing Scenarios

Practice entering new social situations through mock conversations building confidence and skills to forge new connections.

Cognitive Reframing

Challenge negative self-talk calling them burdens, invisible, or trapped to see participation possibilities with support and courage.

Establishing Routines

Integrate regular social activities into weekly schedules. Consistent rhythm builds ongoing engagement, not one-off events.

Encouraging Interdependence

Men must navigate needing assistance from family without sacrificing dignity. Reframing support as courage, not weakness helps.

Discussing Housing Changes

Evaluate when transitioning to senior communities or moving closer to loved ones could provide needed support to reduce isolation's mental health toll.

Uncovering Purpose

Guide isolated men to recognize their wisdom and life experience remain valuable assets they can choose to share with younger generations if they wish to serve others.

Referrals to Support Groups

Peer exchanges reduce isolation by normalizing struggles. Hearing fellow older adults forge bonds despite obstacles inspires pragmatic hope.

Isolation should never be considered natural in advanced age. Simple frictionless onboarding to social ties, reframing self-limiting attitudes and interdependence enable participation and purpose at any age. Courage unites us all.

Chapter 5: Why Men Don't Reach Out For Help

Michael sat across from his wife, Sarah, at the dinner table. She gently brought up concerns that he seemed distant and unhappy over the past few months since losing his job. Michael stared down silently before finally responding, "I appreciate your concern, but I'm fine. Just stressed about work. Don't worry about me."

Inside, Michael felt anything but fine. He was consumed by feelings of failure and worthlessness. But admitting this would mean confronting his depression head-on. Michael had learned long ago that real men handle problems on their own. He was determined not to burden Sarah with his struggles. How could he be a strong provider for the family if he confessed the dark thoughts that crept in unbidden - that she and the kids deserved better than him?

Michael's belief that silent suffering was nobler than seeking help is tragically common among men challenged by depression. This chapter explores the cultural forces and flawed masculine narratives that cause men to isolate themselves, conceal distress, and resist getting treatment and support even in life-threatening situations. Transforming these dynamics is essential to men's mental health.

"I Don't Need Help" - Why Men Avoid Assistance

Our social constructs of masculinity teach boys and men from an early age that demonstrating strength means handling problems independently. Seeking help gets stigmatized as weak and childish. Here are some common thought patterns men invoke to convince themselves support is unnecessary:

"It's not that serious."

Men minimize mental health struggles as temporary setbacks or routine stress they should power through alone. Admitting serious illness contradicts masculine ideals of resilience.

"I'll get through this myself."

This self-reliant mindset derives from cultural messages telling boys to "man up" instead of seeking assistance. Real men tough things out solo.

"Others have it worse."

Comparing themselves to those with bigger problems, men dismiss their own as unworthy of concern. They ignore suffering is subjective, not a competitive sport.

"I don't want to burden anyone."

Men see confiding in loved ones about struggles as a selfish act that drags people down. They convince themselves isolation is noble.

"Therapy is for weaklings."

Many men stigmatize mental healthcare and vulnerability as emasculating failures. It contradicts male ideals of emotional control and strength.

"Medication means defeat."

Admitting needing medication similarly feels like a personal failing for men rather than a routine treatment. Relying only on oneself seems stronger.

Clearly, detrimental cultural programming instills shame and avoidance around men asking for help while equating silent suffering with strength and stoicism. Transforming this damaging mindset constitutes no small task given its deep roots. But progress begins by recognizing the problem.

Beneath the Surface: The Emotions Men Conceal

Societal ideals of manhood teach men to put up a confident, capable front masking inner experiences like:

Sadness

Men feel pressure to uphold an image of steadfastness and invincibility. Admitting sadness feels childlike and pathetic.

Loneliness

The masculine norm of self-reliance leaves men fearing being judged as needy for expressing feelings of isolation and wanting support.

Anxiety

Anxious thoughts contradict ideals of courage and emotional control. Men suppress rumination and uncertainty.

Inadequacy

Struggling with self-doubt or shame doesn't fit the male narrative of continuous confidence and strength.

Helplessness

Men are expected to solve problems decisively on their own. Confessing helplessness violates notions of competence.

Powerlessness

Lacking agency over events undermines ideals of control and dominance expected of men. Such feelings get denied.

Dependence

Needing others contradicts stoic self-sufficiency. Men avoid expressing dependency needs out of masculine obligation.

Vulnerability

Admitting intimate emotions marks the ultimate taboo for men. It risks appearing weak, defenseless and emasculated.

Providing safe outlets for men to acknowledge and constructively discuss these buried feelings and experiences counteracts stigma and isolation. Judging male vulnerability as unmasculine only exacerbates the problem.

The High Costs of Men's Silence

Depression thrives in secrecy. But the toxic masculine beliefs preventing men from opening up about mental health struggles exact steep costs:

Stigma persists: The more men stay silent, the more psychological distress remains stigmatized as weakness in men's eyes. Toxic masculinity continues unchallenged.

Opportunities to intervene early are lost: Men who hide distress until crisis points are missed chances for friends and family to assist before severe consequences like suicide unfold.

Social isolation worsens: Concealing vulnerability out of masculine obligation distances men from vital social support and intervention. Their despair feeds on isolation.

Health deteriorates: Leaving mental illness untreated due to reluctance to show weakness allows clinical depression to manifest through stress disorders, heart attacks, high blood pressure, substance abuse and obesity.

Coping skills stay undeveloped: Avoiding help means men never learn healthy strategies to discuss emotions, handle relationship conflicts, grieve losses and manage work problems. The cycles continues.

Others are reluctant to share: When men stay silent about struggles, it perpetuates the narrative that no other men experience similar issues. Everyone continues hiding.

Clearly, the vast collective costs of men feeling forced into silence about mental health due to cultural constructs demand remedies. New narratives around manhood must take root that encourage openness, support and early intervention without judgment.

Social Barriers That Prevent Men from Seeking Help

Men don't simply wake up one day magically resistant to seeking help. Various societal forces indoctrinate male reluctance over decades:

Early Shaming

When boys express vulnerability, tears or other "feminine" emotions, they often get shamed as weak or immature. Suppressing feelings becomes instinctual.

Toxic Role Models

Fathers, coaches and other male figures modeling hostility towards emotional expression and therapy normalize silence and denial as the manly way to cope.

Media Ridicule

Male characters opening up about insecurities and trauma get mocked as unmasculine in many TV shows and movies. Stigma spreads.

Gender Identity Rigidity

From boyhood, men tie their self-worth to achievement, power, and emotional control. Getting help violates these norms.

Dearth of Male Mental Health Role Models

Unlike sports or business, few mainstream male figures openly discuss therapy, antidepressants, or other mental health treatment to inspire help-seeking.

Lack of Early and Routine Screening

Unlike heart health or diabetes, doctors rarely screen men - especially young or middle-aged - for depression, missing chances for early intervention.

Individualistic Bias

Male socialization emphasize solving problems independently. Admitting need for assistance breaks expectations.

Clearly, reversing men's entrenched mental health stigma requires education, diverse role models and shifts in medical practice - not just preaching self-reliance. No man is an island.

Expanding the Man Box - Healthier Masculinity Norms

Transforming men's reluctance to acknowledge struggles openly and get needed assistance first requires dismantling the constraining "man box" of traditional masculinity norms:

Embracing Emotional Courage

End the shaming of male vulnerability. Encourage boys and men to share full human experience.

Reshaping Strength

Redefine strength as seeking help during challenges, not just stoic self-reliance.

Normalizing Therapy

Eliminate stigma around mental healthcare. Model it as wise self-care, like physical health.

Rewriting Success

Expand limiting definitions of achievement and status beyond work, power and domination.

Valuing Interdependence

Humans need each other. Reframe self-sufficiency as unhealthy arrogance. We all require help sometimes.

Honoring Mentors

Challenge going it alone. Encourage men to seek guidance from role models, counselors, peers and community.

Allowing Imperfection

Demanding perfection pressures men to hide struggles. Have compassion for stumbles as teachers, not failures.

Respecting Rest

Praise men taking breaks and saying no rather than always hustling. Sustainability matters more than grinding.

With consistent modeling of healthier attitudes around masculinity in media, institutions and social groups, men can gradually unlearn mental health stigma and silencing. Now is the moment to speak up.

How Men's Needs Are Overlooked in Mental Health Systems

Beyond social barriers, the modern mental healthcare system itself frequently fails to resonate with men's preferences and needs:

Individualistic Bias

Therapy's emphasis on discussing feelings one-on-one clashes with male preferences for shoulder-to-shoulder doing and group problem-solving.

Medical Model

Psychiatric models labeled men as biologically predisposed towards "weakness". Being the "sick role" contradicts masculine ideals of strength.

Lack of Outreach Tailoring

Outreacharound mental health rarely targets men or addresses masculinity concerns keeping them from accessing services.

Stigma of Diagnosis

Labels like Depression and PTSD deter men who resist perceiving themselves as mentally ill or disordered.

Cost and Access Barriers

With men less likely to have health insurance through employers, high therapy costs often deter help-seeking.

Discomfort With Institutions

Requirements like paperwork, rules, and bureaucracy conflict with male autonomy and independence.

Dearth of Male Providers

The predominance of female therapists alienates some men who would feel more open with male practitioners.

Lack of Anonymity

Confidentiality fears loom large for men in prominent careers where reputation hinges on projecting strength, not "emotional issues".

Medication Stigma

Viewing psychiatric medication as sign of weakness leads many men to resist the very drugs that could help restore mood and functioning.

Transforming mental healthcare culture to welcome men requires profound changes - from trauma-informed training that grasps masculine norms, to anonymous digital options, workplace outreach and male mentorship programs. In time, men will walk through newly opened doors.

Helping Men Transition After Divorce

Divorce deals a crushing blow to many men after the loss of identity, companionship, and family stability. Too often, masculine norms of silence lead men to isolate when they most need support. Here are healthy ways to help men navigate this turbulence:

Listen Without Judgment

Providing a non-judgmental space for men to grieve, process anger, and admit their suffering fosters emotional processing and reduces toxic coping behaviors.

Encourage Journaling

Expressing feelings in writing helps men privately unpack the complex emotions they may initially struggle to voice out loud around loss and despair.

Validate Needs

Affirm wanting comfort, companionship, purpose and stability after divorce as healthy human desires rather than weaknesses. Challenging old stories about masculine self-reliance is crucial.

Check Isolation

Given the masculine tendency to withdraw when hurt, proactively contacting the newly divorced man to keep communication open helps prevent increased isolation.

Offer Practical Help

Providing help in everyday activities such as cooking, transportation, and household repairs alleviates practical challenges when depression makes simple tasks seem overwhelming. Offer concrete support rather than just vague assistance.

Provide Role Models

Introduce divorced men at different stages of growth who have sought help, created healthy social bonds, discovered new purpose and recovered hope. Seeing possibility modeled fosters progress.

Encourage Therapy

Gently challenge notions therapy means failure. Reframe counseling as proactive skills training to healthily process grief, anger and move forward. Combat helplessness.

Suggest Group Support

Group modalities provide needed social connection and learning how other men constructively navigated divorce after isolation subsides.

Confronting divorce's grief openly, reframing help-seeking as wise, and communally reinforcing healthy attitudes provide the scaffolding men require to construct new identities and purpose after the earthquake of divorce. We must offer steadying hands until they stand tall again.

Guy Talk - Men Helping Men Open Up

Due to ingrained mental health stigma and vulnerability aversion in male culture, men often find it easier initially opening up about struggles to fellow men who faced similar issues:

It Starts with One Story

When men break silos and share their authentic stories of getting depression help, it encourages others to open up and realize they are not alone. Vulnerability breeds vulnerability.

Peers Normalize Seeking Treatment

Men who openly discuss attending therapy serve as crucial role models demonstrating that getting professional help aligns with strength, self-care and wisdom - not weakness.

Groups Break Isolation

Male support groups held in locations men already gather, like gyms or veteran halls, provide natural opening to discuss common issues from career changes to divorce that breed depression in male-centric spaces.

Activity Reduces Defensiveness

Conversations during shared hands-on activities - working out, hiking, building projects - often feel safer for men to warm up to taboo topics like mental health without the intensity of direct eye contact.

Humor Diffuses Stigma

Shared jokes and irony help men casually introduce depression and build rapport around formally "off limits" subjects with appropriate humor lowering defenses.

Focus on Skill-Building

Framing groups and counseling as acquiring tools all humans need at times counters avoidance some men have regarding therapy's vulnerable emotional processing.

Establish Confidentiality

Men in prominent careers may resist groups unless settings foster trusted confidentiality, given fears that acknowledging struggle could jeopardize reputation.

Clearly, providing homogeneous male spaces to discuss mental health through shared activities, humor and vulnerability helps traditional support groups reach isolated men afraid to confront depression alone. We all have wounds. Coming together in fellowship lessens the pain until men heal.

Reducing Military Mental Health Stigma

The intensive conditioning of servicemen around strength, stoicism and brotherhood leaves many psychologically unequipped to tackle depression openly without shame. Some ways to reduce military mental health stigma include:

Embedded Providers

Integrating mental health resources seamlessly into primary care settings avoids stigma of going to specialty clinics just for mental illness issues.

Veteran Peers

Having veterans facilitate group sessions and relate concepts like trauma, loss, substance abuse using familiar military imagery reduces defensiveness.

Leadership Culture

Officers prioritizing mental fitness in themselves and subordinates gives "permission" to seek help while spreading awareness that handling stress is a skill to hone like physical training.

Pre-Discharge Outreach

Normalizing mental health checkups as part of the exit process so needs get handled before loss of structure sends floundering vets further into darkness.

Ongoing Community Integration

Veterans groups providing continuity of belonging and purpose after service helps compensate for isolation's trauma-exacerbating effects during re-entry.

Family Education

Informing military families about depression risks and warning signs allows them to intervene with compassion when symptoms manifest, before crises hit.

Respecting Triggers

Educating public venues about avoiding exploding sounds, violent films and trauma-evoking surprises around veterans reduces relapse provocation.

Storytelling as Catharsis

Building safe spaces for veterans to unburden through art, writing workshops and testimony heals isolation's wounds while allowing others to witness without judgment. Their truths deserve light.

With customized approaches reflecting military culture's realities, mindset shifts and skill development emerge organically that encourage distressed service members to constructively address depression before shame leads to tragedy. We owe them this innovation.

Midlife Male Depression - Why It's Underestimated

Unhelpful notions equating midlife dissatisfaction with inevitable decline lead many men struggling at midlife to stay silent rather than admit depression. In truth, middle age brings complex psychological threats to masculine identity:

Physical Changes

Declining strength, endurance and sexual potency contradict cultural masculine ideals centered on vigor, control, and invulnerability.

Career Stagnation

Hitting a plateau professionally around age 40-55 undermines masculine self-image as providers climbing hierarchy ladders to positional power and status.

Economic Pressures

Stagnant incomes failing to match rising family costs for homes, healthcare, college savings and elderly parents strain men's provider identities as traditional breadwinners.

Loss of Youth Bonds

As careers and family obligations take over, men often lose touch with the anchoring friendships forged in school days that provided deeper social intimacy than superficial adult relationships.

Role Confusion

Men who centered their lives around work success and providing materially suddenly feel empty as kids leave home and familiar routines end. Purpose vanishes.

Mortality Fears

Approaching old age triggers existential reflection on death. But men lack outlets to openly discuss these universal human anxieties around life meaning and legacy.

Changing Family Needs

Midlife repression gives way to uncomfortable needs for intimacy, nurturing, and meaning. But men lack models for this emotional growth. Their needs go unmet.

Rather than trivializing midlife distress as inevitable, compassionately understanding these psychological threats through dialogue normalizes men getting help without shame. We all weather storms. Admitting struggle takes true strength.

Why High-Performing Men Face Greater Depression Risk

The cultural script pushing men to tie masculinity to achievement leaves many ambitious, high-performing men profoundly vulnerable to depression. Here are some dynamics behind this paradox:

External vs Internal Identity

Basing self-worth on praise and validation makes men vulnerable to criticism, failure and aging professionally. Depression strikes when the costume of competence slips.

Suppressing Emotions

Climbing the ladder requires emotional control and projecting confidence at all costs. But denying vulnerability breeds emptiness and emotional isolation.

Work Becomes Life

Obsessive overwork leaves no time to nurture social bonds, purpose, intimacy or self-care outside of achievement. Depression brews in the voids.

Comparisons and Competition

Incessantly measuring up against colleagues breeds anxiety and low self-esteem. But admitting inadequacy contradicts the male code.

Perfectionism

Equating minor setbacks at work with personal failure fosters despair and self-blame. Men cannot accept imperfection as part of life.

Loss of Meaning

Climbing socially sanctioned ladders of success leaves many men feeling empty chasing shallow status symbols rather than nurturing community and purpose.

Fear of Revealing Struggles

High-profile men dread exposing mental health battles given expectations to project invincibility. Seeking help seems like professional failure.

Toxic Stress

Corporate culture glorifies insane hours, multitasking, hyperconnectivity at the expense of health. Burnout is the high cost of idealized masculinity.

Poor Coping Skills

Men socialized for competition lack self-care skills to healthily manage setbacks. Unprocessed pain accrues until breaking points.

Clearly, the constant pressure to appear infallible while deriving self-worth externally eventually takes an immense psychological toll. But healing involves learning authentic confidence comes from within, not masking emptiness with achievement. We must teach men this truth.

Why Empty Nest Syndrome Hits Men Hard

When the last child leaves home, depression commonly strikes men who centered their entire masculine identity and purpose around the Provider Father role. What dynamics drive this despair?

Loss of Daily Purpose

With the constant needs of childrearing gone, men lose the vital routine giving structure and meaning to days. A void opens up.

Erosion of Identity

Absent kids to nurture and guide, Dad loses the central activity anchoring his masculine self-image for decades. Confusion follows.

Spousal Disconnection

Without kids as a buffer, couples confront simmering issues avoided earlier. Tensions escalate when communication habits lag.

Career Doubts

As fertility wanes, men question workaholic tendencies that impaired family ties. But voicing regrets seems too late.

Freedom Turns to Boredom

Early retirement dreams lose luster as unstructured time without higher purpose becomes monotonous for men lacking hobbies.

Grandkids Bring Bittersweet Joy

Doting on grandchildren evokes nostalgia for the vitality of hands-on parenting days long gone. Grief emerges.

Financial Burdens

Supporting grown kids' debt and nurturing aging parents create new financial strains at the brink of retirement. Masculine provider esteem suffers.

Mortality Concerns

With their legacy in children now cementing, fears around aging and death grow more urgent and tangible.

Rather than trivializing this distress as just a rite of passage, compassionately understanding these profound losses allows men to grieve while rediscovering passion and meaning to thrive in Act 2 of life.

Why Male Caregiver Depression Goes Unnoticed

Despite the immense stress of full-time caregiving, men tending to ailing spouses or parents rarely confide struggles or access mental health support. What factors perpetuate silent suffering?

Isolation

Housebound without work contacts or peers, solitary male caregivers lack outlets or awareness about sharing burdens. Pride keeps them from "complaining."

Minimizing Stress

Cultural messaging around men's natural talent for leadership and problem-solving makes admitting being overwhelmed feel like profound failure. They downplay issues.

Role Unfamiliarity

Unlike parental duties, hands-on caregiving falls outside expected masculine roles. Men doubt their competence but are ashamed to seek "women's work" help.

Lack of Emotional Skills

Male socialization emphasizes logic over emotional intelligence. But caregiving demands deep wells of compassion men often haven't had opportunities to develop.

Retirement Adjustment

If retirement was recent, the sudden chaos of round-the-clock caregiving obliterates dreams of relaxation. Grieving retirement is socially taboo.

Financial Burden

Few realize caregiving necessitates forgoing paid work. Struggling to pay bills without asking others for help breeds deep shame when masculine identities center on providing.

Displaced Anger

Resentment about the endless needs of ailing parents or partners that erode freedom comes out passive-aggressively. But men feel guilty expressing anger over "duties".

Role Reversal

When robust fathers deteriorate mentally or physically, sons struggle with having to parent their declining patriarchs. Grappling with their hero's mortality feels emasculating.

Clearly, cultural narratives ignore that caregiving poses deep threats to masculine identity around competence, strength, leadership and providing. Safe spaces must open for men to admit these complex griefs without judgment on the isolating caregiver's journey.

Why Midlife Work Struggles Hit Men Hard

Middle age career turbulence like job loss, forced early retirement, or being passed over for promotion lead many men into crippling despair. Let's explore some dynamics behind why midlife work struggles devastate male mental health:

Success Tied to Achievement

Men are conditioned to derive their entire masculine self-image from career victory and breadwinner status. Failure undermines core identity.

Few Non-Work Social Ties

With careers all-consuming, many men lack strong community and family bonds to nurture mental health when work status crumbles. Isolation compounds defeat.

Sudden Identity Erosion

Male esteem built atop a lifetime ladder-climbing is annihilated swiftly when that purpose and social belonging vanishes after job loss.

Financial Devastation

Men laid off are often primary breadwinners struggling to find replacement income to provide for families in a vastly different job market than their outdated skills suit.

Imposter Fears

Being surpassed professionally makes men question if they somehow fooled others into overestimating their talents and worth all these years. Self-doubt snowballs.

Perceived Betrayal

Losing jobs to downsizing after decades of company loyalty feels like an indictment of their character by the organization, evoking bitterness.

Few Role Models

Unlike earlier life stages, few cultural narratives exist around men rebounding positively from major midlife work derailment that breed hope about writing a new story.

Ageism Impacts

Many discarded older workers contend with age discrimination that prevents re-entry despite their sustained skills, forcing earlier unplanned retirement.

Rather than trivialize midlife work loss as routine, we must foster support spaces that allow men to process resulting grief and loss of purpose while rediscovering their value. Every transition, however painful, presents possibilities for renewal.

Why Empty Nest Depression is Different for Dads

When the last child leaves home, depression strikes many fathers who tied their masculine identity to family provider roles. What factors make empty nest transitions uniquely hard for men?

No Social Script

Female empty nest adjustment garners far more cultural understanding. Men feel lost lacking defined behaviors for rediscovering purpose as fatherhood ends.

Spousal Disconnection

Partners often struggle reconnecting after years of childrearing busyness. But men lack skills to articulate relationship needs, fueling isolation.

Undefined Identity

With the paternal role gone, men lose the activity anchoring their masculine self-image for decades. Confusion and aimlessness follow.

Unstructured Time

Early retirement dreams lose luster as unfilled hours without higher purpose become monotonous for dads lacking hobbies or social outlets.

Unmet Needs

Suppressed hurts around career compromises, intimacy losses and aging all reemerge with kids gone. But men lack outlets to discuss these pains.

Unrealistic Expectations

Cultural messaging depicts empty nesters joyfully embracing freedom. Blindsided dads feel ashamed that sadness occupies their empty home instead.

Mortality Fears

Watching kids cement careers and families crystallizes aging finality. But men avoid voicing existential angst around fading youth, vigor and legacy.

Unprocessed Grief

Letting go of cherished paternal bonds kindles multilayered grief. But men are taught to power through emotional pain silently rather than unpack it.

By acknowledging the existential threats empty nesting poses for men rather than minimizing it as an inevitable rite of passage, space opens up to foster resilience, purpose and emotional health for dads braving new crossroads. We must support their transition from Men to Sages.

Why Asking for Help Challenges Male Identity

All humans require assistance at times. But for men trained since boyhood in masculine norms of self-sufficiency, asking others for help counters deeply ingrained self-images. What makes seeking support so challenging?

Burdening Others

Men fear asking for help makes them a nuisance or imposes unfairly on others. They view self-reliance as nobler even if it means suffering alone.

Admitting Weakness

Requiring help gets equated with incompetence or ignorance. Requesting assistance contradicts masculine values like capability and mastery.

Ceding Control

Relying on others means conceding total control over outcomes. Men lose their illusion of independence and power when forced to depend on people.

Nurturing Skills Deficits

If raised in emotionally repressive homes, some men reach adulthood lacking skills to open up to others for nurturing due to lack of modeling. Vulnerability feels alien.

Distrusting Motives

Some men worry offers of support carry hidden expectations of reciprocity. Saying yes means owing favors down the road they would rather avoid.

Fear of Rejection

Under offers of help may lurk social judgments about inadequacy. Admitting needs feels like giving others license to look down on them as unable to cope.

Reliance on Themselves

Habits of solitary problem-solving get reinforced for decades. Even when support exists, men reflexively default to their own headspace rather than include others.

Threat to Status

In career contexts, asking for assistance risks signaling inability to colleagues. Protecting social capital outweighs benefits of collaboration.

By gently challenging these dysfunctional attitudes around self-sufficiency that isolate men, new narratives can take root that frame interdependence and periodic help-seeking as human strengths rather than weaknesses. The lone wolf needs the pack.

Keeping Men from Falling Through the Cracks

Even when mental healthcare access improves, cultural conditioning leads many men to slip through the cracks unless outreach meets them where they are. Here are some gaps where men get lost:

Transition Points

Milestones like new fathers, divorce, retirement, and widowhood breed isolation for men unequipped to form social bonds outside traditional roles. But support lags due to stigma.

High-Functioning Depression

Men maintaining elite careers while depressed avoid treatment to project success. But toxicity festers beneath the façade. Few know to intervene.

Middle Age

Men's midlife physical and emotional needs go unvoiced. By the time depression emerges, isolation is entrenched. They get overlooked, dismissed as typical aging.

Childhood

Before masculinity norms solidify, early intervention helps boys develop emotional skills freely. But few resources for families exist. Missed opportunities abound.

Low-Income and Minoritized Men

Economic and cultural marginalization breed depression but access barriers like cost, racism and complexity deter men seeking government assistance. They suffer silently.

Incarcerated Men

Harsh prison conditions and stigma keep men from utilizing mental health services. Many isolate after release instead of reintegrating into community.

Homeless Men

Shelters and charities lack male-focused services. Pride prevents vulnerable men from seeking scarce resources when they need it most. Their pain stays invisible.

Clearly, technology, innovation and targeted initiatives must be mobilized to reach forgotten pockets of men. We cannot wait for suffering men to find assistance. Compassion must flow to them. Every life hangs in the balance.

Talking to Men About Depression - Dos and Don'ts

Approaching men about possible depression requires nuance and care to overcome avoidance. Here are some guidelines to make sensitive discussions more effective:

DO:

- Listen without judgment or trying to problem-solve immediately.

- Use "masculine" framing like strength, resilience, getting equipped.

- Note changes calmly without confrontation.

- Discuss specific behaviors vs generalizations.

- Align with his values like family duties and work ethic.

- Offer options vs commands.

- Model vulnerability yourself.

- Follow up consistently.

DON'T:

- Minimize symptoms or need for help.

- Threaten ultimatums right away.

- Debate reasons he should not be depressed.

- Tell him to "move past it" or "be strong."

- Corner him unexpectedly.

- Analyze his childhood.

- Make him talk before he's ready.

- Debate treatment approaches initially.

The goal is creating conditions where men feel safe honestly sharing struggles without defensiveness. Have compassion for the fears behind avoidance while building trust consistency, day by unhurried day. Progress unfolds at its own pace when barriers fall away.

Helping Angry Men Get Help

Many depressed men initially present as hostile, irritable and quick-tempered rather than vulnerable. How can caregivers compassionately guide these men toward treatment when anger feels off-putting?

Don't take it personally

Rage often arises from inner shame, not anything you did. Breathe and respond calmly.

Set boundaries without judgment

Anger deserves understanding but misconduct cannot be condoned or enabled. Enforce respectfully.

Note patterns

Rather than reacting to isolated episodes, focus on overall changes like increased outbursts that signal struggling.

Avoid threats and ultimatums

Heavy-handed approaches will be perceived as attacks to defend against. Severing connection must be a last resort.

Interrupt rumination early

Gently redirect fixated venting about perceived past injustices toward problem-solving. Don't let fuming escalate.

Have one-on-one talks

In front of friends or family, angry men feel spotlighted. Speak privately to reduce posturing and increase vulnerability.

Provide space

Pushing for vulnerable sharing right away usually backfires. Let some steam dissipate before delicately checking in again.

Offer activities unrelated to anger

Primitive aggressive energy is cathartic. Suggest intense exercise, focused projects, loud music, or manual labor to channel rage.

Underlying hurt fuels male anger. Avoid demonizing it. With astute redirection and emotional intelligence, caregivers can guide furious men toward healing.

Why Many Men Regret Not Getting Treatment Sooner

As hard as admitting distress and getting help first appears for depressed men, many regret avoiding treatment once hindsight offers clarity about the immense costs of proud silence and isolation:

Relationship Damage

Depression unleashed many interpersonal struggles that hurt loved ones through neglect, missed milestones, emotional absence and anger.

Substance Abuse

Rather than address inner pain, relying on drugs, alcohol and addictive outlets led to health declines and reckless choices.

Wasted Time

Years passed in foggy survival mode just going through motions rather than thriving. Precious life escaped unfulfilled.

Career Setbacks

Work reputation suffered from disengagement, poor focus and constantly using sick days to cope behind the scenes.

Financial Struggles

Men hid money issues bred by impulsive self-medication and inability to perform at work. Too proud to accept pragmatic help, problems multiplied.

Trauma to Kids

Harsh parenting, emotional distance and poor role modeling while depressed inflicted childhood scars for years.

Lost Social Bonds

In the depths of despair, men withdrew from friendships and community ties critical to wellbeing. Reconnection feels hard.

Physical Health Damage

Depression fueled stress disorders, blood pressure spikes, diabetes risks, inflammation, heart problems and weight gain.

Clearly, the false strength of silent suffering ultimately backfired. While humility helps temper regrets about the past, male solidarity should spotlight diverse stories of overdue help-seeking without shame so other men realize timely treatment outshines toxic toughness. We all have lessons to share.

Chapter 6: The Path Forward - Healing Approaches for Men

After examining the cultural forces and masculine norms that compel many men to hide depression behind a façade of stoicism and strength, the question becomes - how can we guide suffering men toward healing? This chapter provides an overview of evidence-based strategies across professional clinical treatment, community-based support, and lifestyle approaches that can help men break free of avoidance and isolation to constructively address depression.

Clinical Therapies Tailored for Men

While medication has a role blending with other solutions, talk therapy remains the most essential first-line treatment for lasting male depression recovery by equipping men with tangible skills to process emotions, transform unhealthy narratives, foster self-compassion and nurture meaningful human bonds. Here are leading therapeutic modalities proving effective with men:

Cognitive Behavioral Therapy (CBT)

By identifying and challenging automatic negative thought patterns fueling despair, CBT helps men dismantle distorted core beliefs like "asking for help means I'm weak" that prevent coping.

Dialectical Behavior Therapy (DBT)

DBT builds critical emotion regulation, communication and distress tolerance skills men often lack due to masculine socialization that dismisses feelings.

Interpersonal Therapy (IPT)

IPT identifies and overcomes relationship struggles through role-playing exchanges, boundary-setting and group feedback to expand men's emotional resources.

Emotionally Focused Therapy (EFT) for Couples

EFT helps men articulate feelings, needs and attachment injuries for healing connection. The structured approach feels "masculine".

Exposure Therapy

This tactic invites men to gradually face fears around vulnerability in a controlled way to increase comfort openly expressing emotions over time.

Mindfulness-Based Therapies

Meditation fosters nonjudgmental awareness of thoughts. This emotional objectivity helps men realize pain is not personal failure. They can let go.

Nature Therapy

Conducting therapy outdoors during activities like hiking, fishing, or gardening aligns with male preferences for hands-on functioning versus just "talking about feelings".

The ideal approach blends modalities to meet individual needs. But the key for men is structuring therapy to feel purposeful and action-oriented in putting in the hard work of healing.

Male Support Groups - Making Vulnerability Contagious

While 1:1 counseling provides critical personalized guidance, group modalities help men realize they are not alone on the path to healing. Shared stories foster hope. Key examples include:

12-Step Groups

Programs like Alcoholics Anonymous not only provide recovery support but male bonding and accountability. Friendships extend beyond the formal sessions.

Divorce Support Groups

Processing the many emotions and practical life changes after divorce requires empathetic peers for men to open up about relationship wounds, identity confusion and rebuilding purpose.

Veteran Peer Groups

Veteran-led meetings allow servicemen to unburden mental health struggles using familiar military cultural references and language. Stigma declines.

Grief Support

Losing a close loved one leaves men reeling but unequipped to express sorrow outside the masculine norm. Communicating grief through creativity or physical activity can help overcome isolation.

Anger Management Classes

With comrades who relate, men learn to channel toxic anger into healthy assertiveness and inner peace through mutual reinforcement.

Outdoor Adventure Therapy

Activities like hiking, camping, fishing and volunteering gets men engaging with peers naturally in the great outdoors while addressing growth and goals.

Workplace Mental Health Groups

Destigmatizing struggles among co-workers helps men avoid silent suffering during job pressures through lived stories of coping and thriving together.

Clearly, group support provides a powerful lifeline for the unique mental health journeys of men. It demonstrates silently struggling is not truly the masculine way. Speaking up and reaching out takes real strength.

Lifestyle Approaches to Improve Men's Mental Fitness

While counseling and community constitute essential foundations in resolving male depression, holistic lifestyle factors also greatly impact mental health trajectories. Some key examples include:

Exercise

cardiovascular activity releases feel-good endorphins while boosting energy, self-image and social outlets with teammates - a powerful depression fighter.

Nutrition

an anti-inflammatory whole foods diet high in Omega-3s, antioxidants and micronutrients equips the body and brain for peak resilience.

Nature Immersion

frequent time outdoors, especially in green spaces, significantly reduces cortisol and rumination while restoring mental balance.

Sleep Hygiene

prioritizing 7-9 hours nightly, limiting devices before bed, and maintaining consistent sleep/wake times bolsters mood through circadian rhythm alignment.

Social Connection

regular informal social activities like sports, volunteering, clubs and gatherings build protective community ties to avoid isolation.

Mindfulness

meditation and breathwork strengthen ability to observe thoughts non-judgmentally, enhancing emotional control.

Journaling

writing exercises allow safe private processing of feelings and experiences that seem too vulnerable to share out loud.

Creative Pursuits

artistic hobbies like music, painting and woodworking provide healthy cathartic outlets for stress and existential angst.

While formal treatment remains essential, proactively surrounding men with daily wellness practices fosters an uplifting lifestyle "ecosystem" that nourishes mental health continually. Sustained recovery requires holistic integration across modalities.

Overcoming Men's Reluctance to Take Medication

Medication serves a vital role in rebalancing brain chemistry for many depression cases. However, given masculine norms valuing self-reliance, many depressed men resist taking antidepressants and other psychiatric drugs. Some ways to overcome this barrier include:

Comparing it to Physical Illness

Framing depression as an illness requiring medicine like diabetes or high blood pressure reduces stigma.

Involving Family in Discussions

Having spouses and loved ones involved normalizes medication as part of comprehensive treatment.

Meeting Men Where They Are

Starting with herbal supplements or therapies like acupuncture can help bridge to prescription drugs later for men leery of biomedical psychiatry.

Monitoring Progress and Side Effects

Check-ins ensure the medication dosage is optimized for symptom relief while minimizing disruptive side effects. This enhances adherence.

Combining it With Lifestyle Actions

Reinforcing daily structure, activity scheduling, and self-care while awaiting drug effects motivates men's sense of partnership in recovery.

Explaining It's Not Forever

Framing medication as a temporary stabilizing tool until therapeutic and lifestyle gains take deeper hold can make long-term adherence more tolerable.

Tapering Up Slowly

Beginning with lower doses that increase gradually helps men adjust to changes in energy, libido or cognition that feel overly jarring when introduced too rapidly.

Ongoing Supportive Accountability

Whether via clinicians, peer groups or loved ones, consistent follow-up encourages men to persist through early uncertainty given masculine tendencies toward avoidance.

With compassionate dialogue and education, men's legitimate concerns about antidepressant use can be unpacked. An integrated biopsychosocial approach centered on meeting men's values and goals fosters needed openness. Healing is a team effort.

Why a Purpose-Centered Approach Matters for Men

One reason depression cuts deeply for men is that it erodes the vital sense of meaning and direction provided by central social roles like careers and family life. Restoring purpose requires existential work:

Rediscovering Passions

Depression often arises when men betray their deep interests to focus excessively on work and achievement dictated by social scripts. Reconnecting to authentic desires kindles motivation and meaning.

Volunteering

Contributing time and energy toward benefiting others breeds satisfaction and perspective, reducing isolation and self-absorption bred by depressive rumination.

Listening to Intuition

Therapists must help depressed men slow down to tune into inner wisdom drowned out for years by judgment, expectations and cynicism. What activities restore calm and clarity?

Values Exploration

What values like justice, community, integrity and service resonate most - outside surface markers of status? Aligning actions with values provides meaning.

Skill Development

Cultivating talents not related to work roles allows men to gain esteem through mastery and purpose during unstructured time like unemployment or retirement when depression risks spike.

Small Group Participation

Joining a book club, support group, recreational team or purpose driven community of belonging allows lonely men to bond through shoulder-to-shoulder action.

Nature Immersion

Being in the outdoors fosters awe and tranquility that provide perspective on what matters most. Men tap into meaning through ocean, forest and sky.

By restructuring days around practices and people that nourish the soul, men move from depressive apathy to vitality rooted in contribution and passions bigger than themselves. No life lacks meaning waiting to be revealed.

Why Work-Centered Men Need Purpose Beyond The Office

Workaholism serves as a socially respected escape for many depressed men avoiding family intimacy and inner growth. But tying masculinity solely to professional achievement proves deeply perilous. What alternatives exist?

Volunteer Work

Giving time to mentor, serve meals, or provide job training offers meaning by supporting those in need through direct contribution.

Caregiving

Caring for aging parents, relatives with disabilities or other dependents builds purpose through compassionate service.

Athletic Goals

Training for marathons, triathlons, weight goals or other athletic feats grounds identity in grit and wellness.

Travel Adventures

Planning meaningful trips oriented around service, learning, culture and nature provides joy and awakening.

Artistic Pursuits

Losing oneself in photography, writing, music and other right-brained outlets fosters growth through creative flow.

Peer Mentorship

Sharing hard-won life lessons and professional skills with younger men trying to build careers allows generous wisdom-transfer.

Home Projects

Refinishing basements, building sheds, gardening and other handiwork grounds men in skill-oriented purpose and legacy.

Continuing Education

Learning new skills, technologies and perspectives prevents stagnation and reminds men of horizons beyond current confines.

Rather than harshly judging work-focused men, compassionately highlight opportunities to broaden identity by embracing purpose that uplifts spirit and community. We all desire to be of use.

Coaching Men to Overcome Isolation

Many depressed men remain disconnected from family, friends, and community due to masculine norms around self-reliance. Here are professional coaching techniques to help overcome isolation:

Assign Conversation Goals

Set objectives like "have one deep conversation weekly" to build emotional intimacy skills through practice.

Teach Communication Tools

Introduce conversation models like "I feel X when Y happens because Z" to foster vulnerability.

Role Play Scenarios

Practicing opening up through mock interactions reduces in-the-moment stress and uncertainty. Confidence builds.

Suggest Icebreakers

Brainstorm casual activities like hiking, playing pool or grabbing coffee that sidestep charged intimacy and facilitate casual chatting to warm up.

Highlight Active Listening

Challenge "silent and stoic" conditioning by teaching reflective listening skills like summarizing, validating feelings, and asking thoughtful questions.

Observe Body Language

Paying deliberate attention to eye contact, posture, gestures and facial expressions during talks builds emotional awareness.

Journal About Fears

Writing to explore fears around vulnerability like loss, shame or burdening others externalizes inner blocks. These can be processed.

Set Intention

Before interactions, committing consciously to drop pretenses, be present and make a connection centers courage to reach out.

By understanding the cultural forces deterring male social participation combined with scaffolded skills training, coaches can gradually guide isolated men back into the embrace of community where their healing awaits. We all long to belong.

Reducing Perfectionism in Depressed Men

The despair of depressed men intensifies when unhealthy perfectionism leads to relentless self-blame over perceived failures. But coaches can shift this by:

Separating Worth From Performance

Help men base self-image on values and character rather than external achievement which breeds burnout.

Allowing Imperfection

Perfectionism destroys joy. Reframing mistakes as universal learning steps reduces shame.

Developing Self-Compassion

Shift critical self-talk to compassionate understanding it arose from childhood factors, not personal defects.

Noting Progress

Focus on effort and improvement rather than demanding immediate success. Small gains matter on the path.

Modifying All-or-Nothing Thinking

Challenge rigid dichotomies like success/failure. Reality operates in grey areas and tradeoffs.

Setting Process Goals

Aiming for incremental learning and engagement makes achievement sustainable long-term versus short-lived end results.

Harnessing Healthy Competitiveness

Redirect competitive zeal from toxic comparisons with others to benign tactics like competing with yesterday's progress.

Modeling Sustainable Effort

Demonstrate pacing, planned breaks and saying no. Men learn overwork does not equate to virtue.

With compassionate understanding of past wounds breeding perfectionism, men can recalibrate exhausting high-achievement compulsion into passionate and purposeful effort that fills the inner void.

Coaching Men Through Destructive Anger

Depressed men frequently harbor intense anger rooted in shame, humiliation and lost control. Coaches can guide catharsis:

Acknowledge Root Pain

Anger detaches men from vulnerability. Help them articulate the hurt beneath rage.

Teach Emotion Regulation Skills

Practicing deep breathing, grounding, counting, and reframing builds tools to pause rage spirals.

Set Healthy Boundaries

Validate anger but enforce misconduct will not be tolerated. Channel it to healthy habits.

Encourage Physical Activity

Intense exercise and recreation provides a vigorous outlet to "burn off" primitive fury.

Assign a Ritual

Develop a routine to symbolize leaving anger behind after productive processing, like lighting a candle or stacking stones.

Cultivate Awareness

Noting physical signs like clenched fists and rigid muscles builds conscious pausing before anger escalates.

Generate Alternatives

Brainstorm non-violent ways to confront situations underlying anger like assertive communication.

Keep a Gratitude Journal

Daily recording small blessings over time shifts perspective from grievances toward life's gifts.

With compassion for the protective role of their anger, men can learn
to honor its message and channel it toward passion and purpose
rather than destruction. Beneath rage awaits deep humanity.

When Therapy Struggles to Reach Men

Due to stigma and norms equating help-seeking with failure, many
depressed men remain averse to therapy's central tenets like
expressing vulnerability and unpacking the past. Some techniques to
overcome resistance include:

Focus on Problem-Solving

Pragmatic guidance for life issues appeals more than exploring
emotions. Once trust builds, feelings follow.

Use Activity-Centered Approaches

Engaging over games, art, or outdoor sessions feels less threatening
than seated talk therapy.

Find Common Interests

Discussing sports, career, parenting - anything masculine - builds
rapport and relevance. Abstract theory distances men.

Ask About Values

What matters to him? Appealing to duty, integrity, loyalty meets
men's orientation to higher purpose.

Avoid Interrogation

Men fear assessment and scrutiny. Warmly sharing your own
experiences reduces power differentials and facilitates openness.

Check Your Biases

Avoid labeling the stoic and silent as inherently toxic. There are
reasons for mistrusting vulnerability. Listen to those.

Accentuate Strengths

Note past examples of perseverance, courage, sacrifice. Men need to know you see their goodness before exposing shame.

Move at His Pace

Resist pressure for emotional breakthroughs. Meet men where they are and build trust. Insights emerge organically over time.

The skilled therapist or counselor artfully blends clinical wisdom with deep respect for the protective role masculine armor historically served. Have faith in men's readiness to heal when finally offered safe harbor.

Group Therapy Guidance for Men

While group modalities provide vital social support, many men resist opening up around others initially. Therapists can foster engagement by:

Explaining Confidentiality

Ensure men no personal details will be shared outside sessions before asking them to be vulnerable. Discretion is imperative.

Starting With Common Interests

Early meetings about neutral topics like sports or movies build rapport. Depression discussions can come later.

Modeling Vulnerability

Leaders showing humanity and fallibility makes transparent sharing feel less threatening.

Moving Slowly

For some men, just listening without participating may be enough first steps. Give space rather than pushing immediate disclosure.

Providing Structure

Agendas, tools and rituals facilitate comfort. Some uncertainty eases when men know what to expect.

Bridging to Individual Therapy

If group sharing remains too daunting, it may open the door to seeking 1:1 counseling. Both are wins.

Tracking Progress

Questionnaires help men see tangible mental health improvements, driving continued engagement.

Managing Conflict

Establish ground rules against put downs. Highlight common humanity during disagreements.

Effective group leaders read subtle cues about each man's readiness and meet him there. Patience and peer bonding foster incremental healing. The path winds gradually upward.

Volunteering - A Powerful Pathway to Healing

Research reveals volunteering significantly boosts mental health and resilience by building community ties and purpose. But cultural stoicism often deters men from participating. Some ways to encourage it include:

Presenting Common Benefits

Highlight research showing volunteering reduces depression, longevity, purpose and social connections.

Tailoring to Interests

Align volunteering with existing passions - like coaching sports, leading veterans groups, or fixing cars. It feels natural rather than imposed altruism.

Starting Small

Have men volunteer just 2-4 hours monthly at first. Over time, these habits cement.

Offering Male-Centered Options

Some men shy away from stereotypically feminine volunteering like reading to kids. Emphasize roles for handymen, coaches and mentors.

Providing Structure

Consistency helps habit-form. Set scheduled days and times to volunteer rather than last minute requests.

Encouraging Companions

Volunteering alongside friends or family makes engagement less intimidating for reluctant men. Camaraderie eases entry.

Noting Health Benefits

Discuss research showing it strengthens immune function, heart health, and cognition - messages that motivate men.

Reframing As Duty

Code volunteering as service to others and community - a calling higher than the self. This aligns with masculine values.

Highlighting Meaning

Contributing one's time and wisdom to benefit others confers a sense of purpose when other foundations like work falter.

Promoting Heroic Models

Spotlight examples of admirable male role models volunteering. This inspires men to follow their example.

Clearly, volunteering's benefits span emotional, physical and spiritual realms. But strategic messaging, habit design and social encouragement optimize chances of motivating depressed men to take that crucial first step beyond loneliness.

Chapter 7: Creating a Culture of Support for Men's Mental Health

While individual men certainly have agency in seeking help for depression, broader cultural forces play pivotal roles shaping attitudes and norms around masculinity, vulnerability and suffering. Just as restrictive rules of manhood fuel male distress, positive systemic change requires us to foster a society where men feel embraced in their full humanity without shame or isolation.

This chapter explores practical steps people can take in their daily lives and relationships to rewrite the story around men's mental health. We focus on public awareness, community resources, institutional policies and media messaging that help boys and men struggling silently feel seen, uplifted and empowered to heal by transforming what "being strong" truly means. The work begins with all of us.

Expanding Public Awareness and Education

Shifting male depression from a hidden epidemic to a normalized issue meriting compassionate dialogue happens through public awareness at all levels. Here are key opportunities to enhance understanding:

School Programs Teaching Healthy Masculinity

From early education onward, lessons about emotional awareness, male trauma, healthy coping and destigmatizing help-seeking lay foundations of vulnerability and literacy. Preventing problems eclipses addressing them reactively.

Workplace Seminars on Men's Mental Health

Trainings on specific conditions like depression, suicide risk factors and available counseling benefits equip co-workers to act as allies reaching out to silently struggling men at early, reversible stages.

physicians about Male Symptoms

Because men often manifest depression differently than women, it is critical to widely educate family doctors, clinics and hospitals on tailored screening tools and warning signs better adapted to male presentations involving anger, violence, substance abuse and escapism. Catching issues early relies on updated diagnostic skills.

Media Campaigns Challenging Masculinity Rules

Programs like the Texas Suicide Prevention Collaborative's "Man Enough" ads depict diverse men opening up to highlight that real strength means acknowledging pain. Humor and role models make messages relatable.

Outreach Through Male Spaces and Events

Tabling at weekend sports leagues, gyms, veterans halls and workplaces builds visibility. On-site activities like free blood pressure checks or stress relief provide natural openings to discuss mental health.

Celebrity Testimonials

Well-known male figures from the worlds of sports, military, business and entertainment speaking candidly about their own therapy, medication and recovery journey powerfully inspire men struggling silently to take heart in knowing they are not alone.

Multipronged public outreach spanning key institutions in men's lives normalizes early help-seeking while challenging outdated scripts equating silent suffering with strength. With consistent visibility about male mental health across ages and settings, real change takes root.

Why Male-Specific Mental Health Services Matter

While not warranting segregation, designated services tailored specifically to men's preferences and needs reduce obstacles many men face engaging with traditional mental healthcare. Some advantages include:

Tailoring Care to Male Norms

Providers trained in masculine socialization and male depression patterns convey understanding and prevent misdiagnoses. Nuanced gender-informed treatment inspires trust.

Peers Provide Familiar Mirrors

Being treated alongside fellow veterans, firefighters or divorced dads reduces stigma. Men open up with those facing similar struggles rather than feeling singled out.

Action-Oriented Approaches

Having therapy and support groups framed as concrete skill-building and equipping to take on life's challenges appeals to masculine preferences for shoulder-to-shoulder action.

Anonymity and Confidentiality

In-person and digital forums allowing men to access help anonymously provide safety to candidly share mental health struggles without occupational or social risks.

Focus on Individual Progress and Goals

Collaboratively tracking progress toward functional goals men value (like work performance or family relationships) incentivizes sticking with treatment plans.

Holistic Health Integration

Merging counseling and peer support with coaching around exercise, nutrition, purpose and mindfulness fosters consistent motivation through lifestyle growth and camaraderie.

Practical Assistance Resources

Case management providing help navigating healthcare systems, transportation, jobs, and caregiving responsibilities eliminates concrete barriers to participating.

The ideal model integrates clinical excellence with deep respect for men's vulnerabilities and masculine perspectives. In time, sufficient public familiarity and success makes male-focused designs no longer imperative - but they are instrumental to bridge current gaps.

Fathers - The Missing Link in Boys' Mental Health Education

Mothers play central nurturing roles in children's lives. But absent involved fathers, boys lack key modeling to develop skills like:

- Handling emotions and setbacks constructively

- forming intimacy and trusting bonds

- pursuing passions with modulated discipline

- standing up to harmful peer pressure

- communicating assertively and resolving conflicts

- being a steward for family and community

- caring for self and others holistically

- breaking limiting intergenerational patterns

Consciously participating in boys' lives prepares them for well-rounded masculine adulthood. Fathers model that true men walk with steady strength through both joy and storms. Their light guides boys forward.

Improving Academic Accommodations for Student Mental Health

Rigid educational environments often fail boys and young men experiencing untreated depression and trauma during crucial development phases. More student supports could help them thrive:

Staff Trainings on Male Mental Health

Equipping teachers to recognize symptoms like social withdrawal, substance abuse, bullying and anger provides needed empathy to understand boys' distress as illness - not willful misconduct.

Enhancing School Counselor Resources

Expanding counselor-student ratios allows time to build key mentoring relationships and equip boys with healthy social-emotional tools they may lack at home.

Flexibility Around Grades and Deadlines

Accommodating mental health setbacks with extensions or exceptions communicates support. Punitive rigidness during crises breeds shame and isolation.

Peer Guidance Programs

Students supporting fellow students fosters community. Allowing boys space to be heard counters conditioning discouraging vulnerability as weakness.

Virtual Class Options

Remote learning alternatives for students needing time away provide inclusivity. Mental health should not force boys to put education on hold indefinitely.

Meditation and Therapy Breaks

Wellness spaces to decompress during high-stress periods normalize pausing rather than grinding endlessly. Cultural change starts small.

With innovations to foster belonging, boys gain foundations to process struggle in ways society often inhibits. Their worth exceeds grades and conformity. Schools can illuminate the way.

Reducing Men's Healthcare Cost Barriers

Cost deterrence poses a huge barrier to men seeking therapy and psychiatric care. Some solutions include:

Free Clinic Networks

Low-cost and volunteer-run community health centers reduce financial hurdles to both physical and mental healthcare. No one should suffer without treatment due to affordability.

Workplace Mental Health Benefits

Ensuring insurance plans equally cover therapy, psychiatry and medications makes out-of-pocket expenses less prohibitive for working men to get help.

Sliding Scale Options

More therapists offering flexible costs based on income like $25 per session broadens access for uninsured and lower-wage men.

Online Lower-Cost Providers

Virtual therapy expands affordable availability. Digital options from $30-65 per week bring counselors into men's homes conveniently.

Medication Assistance Plans

Pharmaceutical firm programs providing free or discounted prescription drugs prevent cost barriers to mental health stability. But ease of access and awareness remains limited.

Government Subsidies

Policymakers should expand funding for clinics providing free behavioral health services with few qualification restrictions in underserved communities.

Insurance Mandates

Requiring plans to include generous, unlimited mental healthcare alongside physical coverage makes parity a right, not luxury.

Systemic changes closing cost gaps inhibiting men from seeking treatment ensure everyone can access their human right to mental well-being.

Changing Media Representations of Masculinity

Given media's profound cultural influence, responsible portrayals of masculinity provide vital modeling. Some ways to break limiting stereotypes include:

Mutual Caring Between Men

Showing genuine affection and emotional intimacy in male friendships and family relationships models vulnerability as natural - not emasculating.

Men Exploring a Full Range of Emotions

Characters grappling with doubt, sadness, confusion, anxiety and hurt in realistic ways teaches boys it's healthy to express emotions.

Addressing Depression, Grief and Trauma

Thoughtfully depicting men recovering from loss through professional help and community support provides familiar narratives boys can internalize.

Healthy Conflict Resolution

Scenes of men engaging in constructive communication during conflicts present alternatives to repression or aggression.

Nonviolent Male Mentorship

Caring fathers, teachers, uncles and coaches guiding boys through emotional struggles with patience counters rigid norms equating manhood with toughness.

Men Participating in Child Rearing

Involved, expressive fathers normalizes that caregiving and domestic participation complement masculine identity.

Men Forming Healthy Intimate Relationships

Portrayals of mutually supportive couples communicating through tension provides models for boys to emulate.

Media makers have a responsibility to thoughtfully expand restrictive masculine stereotypes that fuel stigma and suffering when boys playback those social scripts in their own lives. We all learn from stories. Better tales must be told.

Promoting Social Support in Male Spaces

Support depends on social ties. But masculine environments often inhibit vulnerability. Some ways to cultivate bonding include:

Peer Support During Life Transitions

Divorce care groups at churches, retirement preparation classes, new father bootcamps - targeted aid during stressful transitions builds communal tools to weather challenges.

Veterans Groups for Camaraderie

Ongoing informal gatherings at VFW halls, community centers and coffee shops provide continuity beyond clinical treatment to sustain hard-won recovery.

Activity-Centered Father Gatherings

Organizations fostering hands-on father-son playtime, outings and service opportunities strengthen bonds lacking in many men's lives.

Workplace Wellness Programs

Demystifying mental healthcare through funded counseling, stress relief activities and men's support groups at work reduces stigma and isolation among colleagues.

Online Men's Forums

Anonymous digital community spaces allow isolated men to safely open up about stigmatized struggles to receive understanding they may lack locally.

Informal Social Spaces and Clubs

Just being together in comforting shoulder-to-shoulder rituals like sports teams, fraternal organizations, craft beer nights and game evenings strengthens social rootedness.

Mentoring Programs

Boys need role models demonstrating healthy masculinity. Volunteer mentorships provide intergenerational ties and wisdom transfer.

Programming fostering community helps men cultivate emotional intelligence and mutual aid organically by learning vulnerability is merely human. Over time, support is no longer taboo.

Training Clinicians in Men's Mental Health Nuances

With different symptomology and barriers than women, properly identifying and compassionately treating men's mental illness requires niche clinical skills like:

Familiarity With Male Depression Patterns

Anger, aggression, substance abuse, sexual dysfunction and escapism often disguise male despair. Spotting camouflaged symptoms prevents missed diagnoses.

Accounting for Reluctance and Minimizing

Men frequently downplay symptoms and avoid help-seeking. Clinicians need patience and skill building trust/rapport despite initial wariness.

Assessing Self-Destructive Behaviors

Risky conduct, daredevil acts, recklessness and self-neglect may signify men detaching from hope and self-worth as depression worsens.

Framing Treatment as Restoring Control, Purpose and Functioning

Positioning therapy outcomes in active, pragmatic and instrumental terms aligns with masculine preferences better than exploring feelings abstractly.

Starting Where Men Are.

If emotions feel off-limits initially, focusing on work, family, life satisfaction and strengths meets men subtly over time for incremental sharing when ready.

Preventing Early Dropout

Men tend to resist medication side effects or lengthy talk therapy. Offering achievable markers of progress and variety sustains engagement.

Monitoring Risks of Silence

Reminding men vulnerability is courage not cowardice is key where stigma prevents discussing abuse, trauma, suicidal thoughts. Barriers cause casualties when unaddressed.

With specialized outreach respecting masculine perspectives, clinical services can transform from intimidating institutions into indispensable guides fostering hope and understanding on the path to wholeness.

Launching Targeted Men's Mental Health Outreach

Mainstream mental health promotion often fails to capture men's attention and interests. But tailored outreach meeting men where they are shows promise:

Gender-Specific Messaging and Materials

Campaigns depicting honest portrayals of men receiving help successfully challenge limiting stereotypes. Relatable stories spur action.

Events and Activities at Male Gathering Places

Gyms, military bases, college dorms, sports bars - bringing resources to existing community hubs builds trust.

Virtual Platforms Geared for Men

Apps, online forums, text-based helplines provide anonymity. Digital spaces are accessible gateways.

Focusing on Functionality and Strengths

Framing treatment as restoring purpose and control (not emotional catharsis) dispels stigma around being "weak".

Partnerships with Respected Male Leaders

Outreach involving clergy, coaches, veterans carries credibility and social permission giving men "permission" to seek assistance.

Skills-Building and Problem-Solving

Education on health practices like exercise, sleep, nutrition and stress management feel active versus passive treatment.

Anonymous Assessments

Confidential screeners at events remove self-identification fears but begin quantifying local mental health needs. Awareness flows from data.

Thoughtfully designed outreach meeting men's preferences - not predetermined clinical norms - promises to enhance familiarity, utilization and outcomes for male mental healthcare. We must go outside the box to bring them in.

Improving Male Mental Health Literacy

Despite rising awareness, significant gaps and myths around mental illness persist in the mainstream. Some ways to foster accurate public understanding include:

Explaining It's not "Just Stress"

Educate how clinical mood disorders differ from temporary distress. Biology, thought patterns, functioning and duration set them apart.

Note Prevalence in All Populations

Spotlight data showing depression affects males across all ages, ethnicities, personalities and backgrounds - it is no one's fault or failing.

Clarify Causes are Multi-Factorial

Illustrate the interplay between genetic, hormonal, environmental and trauma factors underpinning mental illness rather than oversimplifying origins.

Share Stories of Recovery

Real testimonials about treatment journeys from everyday men foster hope about depression not being permanent, mysterious or "untreatable".

Note Signs and Symptoms

Increasing awareness of "red flags" like agitation, recklessness, hypersomnia and substance abuse makes early intervention possible before crisis.

Frame as Any Other Illness

Describe mental healthcare matter-of-factly as medicine, just like cardiology or oncology, to dismantle stigma of "shrinks" and "happy pills".

Highlight Holistic Health Connections

Draw links between mental fitness, physical activity, sleep, nutrition and community bonds that underscore roots of wellbeing beyond medicine alone.

With improved public understanding, outdated assumptions painting mental illness as personal weakness rather than complex phenomena open pathways to compassion and healing. Knowledge disarms stigma.

Promoting Workplace Mental Health for Men

Workplace stress affects millions but self-reliance norms keep many men suffering silently. Some promising support strategies include:

Leadership Endorsing Help-Seeking

Executives openly modeling work-life balance, taking vacations/sick days without shame, and appreciating colleagues preventing burnout fosters cultural change.

Mental Health Days

Allowing allotted paid days off specifically for emotional health without needing excuses reduces presenteeism and unsustainable overwork among men.

Peer Support Groups

Employees dealing with similar stresses like new fathers, midlife career concerns, substance abuse, and marital issues can anonymously support one another.

Managers Trained in Mental Health First Aid

Learning compassionate response skills, warning signs, and company resources equips leaders to support struggling employees early.

EAPs and Confidential Counseling

Robust employee assistance programs providing affordable access to therapy, family counseling, addiction treatment and crisis aid should be actively promoted.

Mindfulness Programs

Meditation and emotional intelligence classes during work hours help male employees build healthy coping skills amid workplace demands.

Voluntary Mental Health Check-ins

Optional annual screening interviews with counselors allow men to discuss struggles without judgement before they reach critical points.

Work-Life Blending

Normalizing periodic flexible schedules, remote work and reduced hours smooths juggling professional and family responsibilities before they become untenable.

Proactive strategies prevent many crises reaching tipping points. Comprehensive workplace mental health support promises triple bottom line returns - for employees, families and profitability.

Launching Community Resilience Programs for Boys

Equipping boys early with emotional skills and diverse interests fosters resilience. Some impactful approaches include:

Social-Emotional Learning

Curricula building self-awareness, healthy communication, stress management and empathy prevents struggles from festering silently.

Mentoring Programs

Caring adult mentors help boys construct positive identity foundations and make wise choices during turbulent adolescence.

Recreational Outlets

Free youth sports leagues, camps, music programs and clubs allow boys to discover passions and belonging.

Parenting Workshops

Classes helping moms and dads nurture emotional intelligence, model vulnerability and discipline constructively provide missing family foundations.

Support Groups

Peer gatherings fostering safe discussions about shame, bullying, isolation and other struggles helps boys realize they are not alone. Healing happens together.

Counseling

Proactively making counselors available normalizes seeking help early before adolescent troubles cascade.

Drug and Alcohol Education

Beyond scare tactics, thoughtful evidence-based prevention programming gives boys tools to navigate peer influences and destructive escape impulses.

Rites of Passage Ceremonies

Programs guiding boys to reflect deeply on purpose, character and community as they transition into adulthood foster emotional intelligence and wisdom.

With adequate nurturing, mentorship and modeling of healthy masculinity, young men gain tools to construct lives of purpose and connectedness. Our greatest resource lies in how we raise our sons.

Reducing Men's Homelessness - A Mental Health Crisis

Homelessness leaves already struggling men isolated and without resources to address underlying trauma, addiction and despair. Some reforms include:

Low-Barrier Shelters

Meeting basic safety needs without imposing sobriety, medication, IDs or other deterrents helps desperate men stabilize so formal treatment becomes possible.

Outreach Mental Health Teams

Proactively delivering psychiatric services, medication, therapy and social work on the streets builds trust to transition chronically homeless men into care.

Permanent Supportive Housing

Providing long-term affordable housing with wrap-around services fosters consistency and community men need to maintain recovery.

Skills Training

Equipping homeless men with social-emotional tools alongside vocational coaching builds self-efficacy and purpose necessary for re-entering society.

Transitional Jobs Programs

Subsidized temporary employment helps homeless men re-acclimate to structured work and start rebuilding career pathways.

Male Survivors Support

For homeless men with histories of trauma and abuse, specialized clinical and peer support helps break cycles tormenting body and soul.

Family Reunification

For those open to reconciliation, facilitation services can mend broken relationships providing essential support networks.

Ongoing Case Management

Continuity of care management ensures highly mobile homeless men follow through with mental health, medical and other appointments during the fragile transition back into housing and work.

Comprehensive interventions focused on healing trauma and developing skills, not just providing shelter, equips homeless men to rewrite their narratives from despair to purpose. But political will and resources remain lacking.

Helping Men Transition After Incarceration

The extreme isolation of prison breeds mental health crises. But supportive re-entry programs show promise:

Inside Counseling and Therapy

Access to quality counseling, support groups and anger management inside facilities plants seeds for further growth after release.

Medication Consistency

Preventing disrupted psychiatric medication and care during churn of transfers and release stabilizes inmates with serious mental illness.

Life Skills Training

Equipping men with practical knowledge around finances, healthcare, transportation, housing and vocational skills bolsters self-efficacy.

Transitional Facilities

Supervised group homes allowing former inmates to gradually reintegrate cultivates community and aids re-habituation into society.

Job Readiness Programs

Vocational coaching, internships and mentoring build work capacity, confidence and purpose.

Addiction Support Networks

Fellowships, counseling and sponsors steer ex-inmates away from substance abuse relapse and toward social participation.

Mentorship

Role models provide empathy and living proof that overcoming past mistakes is possible. Their belief kindles hope.

Family Counseling

Navigating complex relationship dynamics after incarceration requires skill-building for all parties via therapy focusing on trust, forgiveness and boundaries.

The re-entry journey is filled with obstacles, but men thrive when given adequate staffing, resources and social scaffolding. Their potential should never be discounted or abandoned.

Preventing Men's Suicide Through Lifestyle Medicine

While psychotherapy and medication remain first-line treatments, holistic wellbeing practices also show measurable anti-suicide benefits:

Physical Activity

All types of exercise robustly reduce depression, aggression and suicidal thoughts by releasing feel-good endorphins and boosting self-efficacy.

Nutrition

Anti-inflammatory diets high in Omega-3s, antioxidants, fiber and key micronutrients equip the brain for resilience and optimal neurotransmitter function.

Nature Immersion

Time outdoors - especially in green spaces - significantly lifts mood and reduces rumination by lowering cortisol and inducing calm.

Stress Management

Meditation, massage, float therapy and controlled breathing counteract anxiety, muscular armoring, cognitive distortions and hopelessness.

Social Connection

Loneliness and isolation underscore suicide risk. Shared activities, volunteering and community integration foster belonging.

Meaning and Purpose

Channeling energy into service, creativity, athletics, spirituality or family life grounds the mind away from destructive thoughts.

Adventure Therapy

Outdoor high thrill activities conducted in groups induce bonding, mindfulness, resilience and confidence to thrive through adversity.

Faith-Based Support

For religiously-inclined men, spiritual counsel and rituals affirm existential worth and interconnectedness beyond the material world.

While not replacing clinical care of serious mental illness, integrated lifestyle approaches have synergistic anti-depressant and anti-suicide benefits that empower men to reclaim wholeness. The light inside reignites.

Helping Men Rediscover Meaning and Purpose

A sense of meaninglessness often incubates male depression. How can men cultivate purpose amid loss and uncertainty? Some pathways:

Explore Existential Questions

What legacy to leave behind? What wisdom to pass on? What matters beyond status and achievement? Life's purpose frequently hides in plain sight.

Get Back to Nature

Time in forests, mountains, oceans and deserts puts problems in perspective and reminds that each life plays a role in the planet's eternal cycles.

Help Others

Volunteering to assist people facing poverty, disability, or neglect builds empathy and connection - the antidote to isolation.

Build Something

Creating works of craftsmanship, art or community enrichment imbues pride and reveals creativity beneath corporate roles.

Nurture Bonds

Depression withers in loving family and friendship circles. Simple shared moments matter more than grand achievements.

Learn and Grow

Cultivating mastery in any skill or domain - from cooking to carpentry to quantum physics - challenges stagnation.

Find Flow States

Lose yourself in passionate pursuits like music, athletics, gardening. Time dissolves when mind, body and spirit synthesize in activity.

Live Your Values

As other foundations crumble, deciding to live each day aligned with your highest ethical principles anchors inner peace.

The light of meaning shines within each of us, however dimmed. When purpose fades, legacy, bonds, service and principles endure to guide the way. We walk this road together.

Promoting Work-Life Balance for Men

Long work hours and constant connectivity fuel male burnout and emptiness. Some solutions include:

Paid Vacation Minimums

Guaranteeing 4-6 weeks annual paid time off by law allows men refreshing breaks without income loss or stigma.

Sick Day Allowances

Separating allotted mental health days from regular sick leave helps men take time off for emotional needs without pretending physical illness.

Work Hour Limits Caps on excessive overtime ensures men have energy left for family and self-care. Workaholism breeds depression.

Email Management Expectations Policies limiting after-hours work communication and requiring genuine time off relieves burnout.

Remote Work Options Flexible location choices permit balance between career and caregiving without sacrifices.

Paternity Leave Equal family leave for fathers strengthens bonding and co-parenting. Kids need present dads.

Gratitude Practices Managers encouraging team wellbeing through appreciations, mediations and affirmations at meetings shifts toxic hustle culture.

Mandatory Retreats Multi-day company-sponsored self-care retreats emphasizing community, nature, art and reflection renew meaning.

Work should energize, not exhaust, the human spirit. Protecting men's right to balance and renewal apart from careers allows warm community bonds to take root in the spaces where industry cannot tread. Life is nourished by purpose, not productivity alone.

Building a National Men's Mental Health Movement

Despite rising awareness, male despair remains an underestimated public health crisis warranting high-level coordination, funding and political will. Some national initiatives could include:

Office of Men's Health

Mirroring the vibrant Office of Women's Health, an agency researching male-specific illness and directing public outreach would formalize efforts.

Congressional Men's Health Caucus

A nonpartisan coalition advancing policy solutions around male suicide, depression, trauma, and incarceration could break gridlock.

Boys' Emotional Education Federal Standards

Creating social-emotional learning benchmarks for schools to receive certain funding would foster vulnerability and coping skills to prevent mental illness.

Workplace Mental Health Incentives

Tax credits encouraging comprehensive employee counseling benefits and peer support programs would enhance early treatment access where men spend much of their time.

First Responder Mental Health Research

Targeted studies on depression, PTSD, suicide and stigma in male-dominated vocations like police, fire, military and emergency medical services would guide support.

Male Healthcare Discrimination Protections

Closing loopholes allowing insurers to exclude coverage for mental health services would enforce parity and access.

Public Health Awareness Campaigns

Advertising campaigns supported by the CDC, such as the effective "Real Men. Real Depression," could be consistently broadcast on sports networks and other platforms where men gather, encouraging them to seek help.

Suicide Hotline Funding

Expanding the National Suicide Prevention Lifeline's capacity and marketing to ensure 24/7 support reduces barriers to men initiating outreach.

Elevating male mental health as a national priority backed by resources would seed a societal shift away from shaming vulnerability toward embracing human wholeness. We all benefit when the suffering find solace.

Immigrant Men - Vulnerabilities and Support

Male immigrants wrestle unique depression challenges from isolation, economic instability, identity crises and discrimination:

Pre-Migration Traumas

Many come fleeing violence, disasters, persecution and other losses that already induce PTSD vulnerability. Stability crumbles.

Lack of Documentation

Constant threat of detention and deportation paralyzes undocumented men who fear seeking public assistance will expose families.

Downward Mobility

Despite high credentials, many only find grueling manual labor in their adoptive country. Shame and despair follow.

Language Barriers

Navigating systems, caseworkers and landlords proves daunting for men still learning English. Even small tasks feel impossible.

Family Separation

Spouses and kids often remain in home countries until immigration systems slowly reunite households. Loneliness takes a toll.

Discrimination and Xenophobia

Marginalization from wider society through bigotry and "othering" impairs self-worth and trust.

Loss of Male Privilege

In nations with greater gender equality, immigrant men feel threatened losing patriarchal household authority possessive of traditional masculinity.

Lack of Citizenship Pathways

Living in limbo without pathways to legal permanent status breeds chronic anxiety and instability. Men feel powerless.

Creating welcoming environments for immigrant men to access care, build communal ties and maintain cultural traditions fosters esteem and hope amid Gaussian transitions. All seek dignity.

Male Depression in Minority Ethnic Groups

Diverse men wrestle amplified depression burdens from discrimination and cultural conflicts:

African American Men

- Mental healthcare stigma runs high in Black communities

- Economic barriers hinder treatment access

- Racism erodes self-worth insidiously

Native American Men

- Depression intrinsically ties to cultural genocide and loss

- Remote reservations lack resources

- High rates of alcoholism and suicide call for tribe-based healing

Asian American Men

- Cultural norms stifling emotional expression deter help-seeking

- Saving face prevents admitting struggles

- Intergenerational family conflict breeds isolation

Latino Men

- Machismo norms foster flawed invincibility concepts

- Poverty, exploitation, and oppression fuel helplessness

- Documentation status blocks care access and powerlessness

Healing must address root causes of identity, powerlessness and trauma. Dismantling barriers to help-seeking empowers minority men to access their inner wisdom and resilience.

Partnering with Faith Groups to Support Men

Many spiritually-oriented men living with depression turn first to religious communities. Some ways congregations can assist include:

Mental Health Ministries

Support groups, counseling referrals and seminars hosted at churches reduce stigma through mingling spiritual and psychological care.

Clergy Mental Health Training

Equipping ministers to recognize symptoms, provide empathetic listening and build inclusion allows them to compassionately guide struggling men.

Spiritual Outreach

Counselors versed in religious scriptures and rituals earn men's trust to improve adherence by framing therapy through a faith lens.

Congregation Awareness

Preaching on mental health and stories of congregants recovering reduces shame. People support what they understand.

Rituals for Healing

Ceremonies fostering grief expression and requesting community aid provide catharsis within familiar traditions.

Prayer and Scripture

Personal spiritual practices or faith-based workbook exercises nourish existential healing for religious men alongside clinical treatment.

Service Opportunities

Volunteering and activism nurtures purpose for men questioning their worth after setbacks.

With deeper understanding of psychology among clergy and mental health incorporating spiritual tools when appropriate, faith communities and clinicians can symbiotically guide men through darkness into light.

Ending the Silence - Voices of Male Mental Health Advocates

The cultural narratives surrounding manhood that isolate depressed men from support will only transform when courageous men break taboos by sharing their own stories. Amplifying diverse voices accelerates change. To men afraid to speak up, consider:

- Your story may inspire fellow silent sufferers to seek help. You could save lives.

- Opening up normalizes men's mental health challenges as shared human experience, not shameful secrets.

- Your vulnerability helps rewrite restrictive rules of manhood that prevent boys from maturing into full humanity.

- Speaking truth dissolves stigma, floods dark corners with light, and builds courage in other men's hearts.

- Even if your voice shakes, your message has power. Your authentic truth sets other men free.

- Our short time on earth is better spent uplifting each other than keeping secrets to comfort the ignorant.

- What is grief, if not love preserving itself from total loss? Honor those who remain by kindling hope.

- When communities unite to care, isolation dissolves. The windows where light enters are infinite.

- Your life lessons equip you to guide others from despair to purpose. We need your vision.

- If not you, then who? Every day, the quiet heroes among us lead the way forward through pain's fertile ashes. It starts with one voice, then another. Speak.

The stories whispering inside you carry wisdom our world needs. Letting them fly on courageous wings lifts all humanity higher. We suffer alone, but heal together.

Conclusion: Bringing Men in from the Cold

We have explored the vast, silent epidemic of depression plaguing millions of men worldwide. Throughout this journey, the overarching theme remains clear - restrictive cultural rules around masculinity serve to isolate men within their own minds and bodies, severing human bonds that give life meaning.

Suffering alone contradicts our deepest nature. As social creatures, we thrive through shared stories that testify to our collective yearning for purpose and belonging. Yet traditional constructs of manhood mock such vulnerability as weakness, leaving depressed men to silently shoulder layers of shame, anger and despair.

Behind the mask of invincibility resides every man's core need for compassion, understanding and connection. But the armor insulates men from the very warmth that kindles lasting peace. So the toll compounds over years as families sorrowfully watch men withdraw into hellish inner landscapes they desperately wish to understand, but cannot penetrate.

We all have absorbed limiting narratives about manhood, strength and maturity that compel silence and disconnection. Transformation begins by bringing these forces into the light of conscious awareness. We must challenge stories that imprison men in callous cages of cold, hard perfectionism. Cultural healing starts with ruthless truth-telling - and the courage to rewrite masculine norms that destroy life rather than nurture it.

The Way Forward

How do we chart a new course that guides men out of the lifeless limbo between phantom strength and vulnerability? The solutions are nuanced but clear:

We must foster a culture that honors the full spectrum of human emotions as normal rather than shaming vulnerability as feminine or childish. Boys require mentors who model healthy outlets for stress, loss and hurt without judgment.

All men need permission to openly explore uncertainty, pain and growth without social penalties or loss of respect. This requires radical redefinition of concepts like toughness, maturity and power across all the institutions shaping male identity from boyhood onward.

And men who model the extraordinary courage required to ask for help, process trauma, shed tears, admit mistakes and mend brokenness deserve our admiration - not scorn. Their strength blossoms by uniting the mind, body and spirit torn asunder by stifling rules of manhood.

Healing also requires practical expansion of mental healthcare resources tailored to support men's preferences and values. Outreach should meet men where they are, framed as equipping for life's challenges with pragmatic skills rather than nebulous exploration of feelings. Therapists serving men require specialized training in masculine norms and barriers that keep silent suffering sacrosanct.

Holistic help exists for those ready to take the hand extended in solace. But first, we must kneel eye to eye with suffering men, validate why vulnerability feels threatening amid a lifetime of messaging distorting emotional expression as unmasculine. Their walls make sense; barbed wire seemed the sole defense from a harsh world's judgments.

With persistence and care, though, even the most solid fortress unlocks from within when the frightened, exhausted soul behind it realizes sincere freedom and community await on the other side. If we cannot shatter the walls, we can unlock the door.

The Journey From Boys to Men

Fundamentally, our task is shepherding boys into an expansive definition of masculinity centered on purpose and service rather than status and power. This calls us to:

- Guide boys in exploring emotions safely through modeling, mentoring and coaching. Do not shame emotional awareness as weak, but welcome it as wisdom.

- Expand adolescent social-emotional education beyond just academics and physical fitness. Teach boys cognitive flexibility, relationship skills, mindfulness of thoughts, stress management, and moral development.

- Encourage creative arts, poetry, dance, literature and spirituality as equally valid outlets for boys alongside traditional sports to foster diverse expressions of self.

- Make counseling and peer support groups available at schools and youth organizations without stigma. Early intervention prevents problems worsening silently.

- Discuss mental health openly at home and normalize help seeking by taking boys to family therapy. Do not isolate boys in the name of self-reliance.

- Frame manhood as defined by purpose-driven legacy built through compassion, human dignity and care for others. The world needs their light more than stoicism.

With consistent warm guidance, boys develop into men rich in emotional wisdom, authenticity and wholeness. But first we must expand the walls of manhood's prison to reveal possibilities beyond. Our sons can be so much more.

Transcending the Mask Together

In truth, all human beings don masculine and feminine masks by turns. We deny and silence aspects of ourselves to comply with social ideals or avoid vulnerability and shame. But the cost is alienation from our hidden wholeness.

Healing is possible when we help men look behind their masks without judgment to find common ground in our shared human struggle to be seen and loved as we are. If we cannot shatter every mask, perhaps we can loosen its constraints with compassion. Behind each façade lies a story aching to be told, and a spirit awaiting permission to live unbound by fear.

So let us have faith in men's inherent goodness waiting to be unveiled. Someday, the masks may grow so light that the wearer forgets they are even there. Till then, we walk alongside men when the path ahead seems too dark to endure alone. Together, step by step, we carry hope sealed inside all human hearts that someday every mask will fall away for good.

When men stop performing manhood and instead rest in their humanity, when strength is measured by courage to be vulnerable rather than ability to dominate, when masculinity expands into wholeness - our collective healing will be at hand.

May we live to witness the day.

About the Author

Dr. Monday Farouq is a psychologist and Medical Rehabilitation specialist who has dedicated his career to unraveling the complexities of the human mind and spirit. With over 20 years of experience, his insightful new book "Behind the Mask: Understanding and Healing Male Depression" represents the culmination of his life's work helping individuals find inner peace and mental well-being.

Born in Lagos, Nigeria, Dr. Farouq's passion for understanding the human condition blossomed at an early age. He earned bachelor's and master's degrees in psychology and furthered to earn a Ph.D. in Clinical Psychology.

After graduating, Dr. Farouq worked in community mental health clinics serving disadvantaged minorities, veterans, and incarcerated populations. During this formative clinical experience, he became acutely attuned to the unique barriers keeping depressed men isolated and untreated. Farouq noticed patterns of profound pain and vulnerability lurking beneath the false masks of masculine strength and stoicism. He made it his life's purpose to help men break free of toxic conditioning and unearth their humanity.

In addition to his therapy practice, Dr. Farouq has spent the past decade conducting field research on contributors to the rising male mental health crisis across age, ethnic and socioeconomic demographics. He has published influential papers in peer-reviewed psychology journals about masculine norms, depression stigma, suicidality and barriers deterring men from treatment.

However, Farouq remained unsatisfied confining his discoveries to academic circles. He wrote "Behind the Mask" to share psychological insights with the general public in an accessible, compassionate style. Blending clinical expertise with men's real stories of hardship and healing, Farouq aims to de-stigmatize male mental illness while providing a practical roadmap for living with purpose beyond outdated masculine expectations.

Also, a father of boys himself, Dr. Farouq feels a profound personal urgency to his work reshaping cultural narratives surrounding manhood. It is his dearest hope that the wisdom in "Behind the Mask" helps create a more just, emotionally intelligent and empathetic society for generations of men to come. By recognizing our shared struggles and cultivating compassion, he believes humanity can emerge from despair into the light of our full potential. The future remains unwritten, as Farouq continues striving to rewrite the story of masculinity with his groundbreaking research, counseling, writing and mentorship.